PRAISE FOR SOME KISS WE WANT

These astonishing poems in Dorothy Walters' "Some Kiss We Want" are at once a revelation and an incantation, humble and illumined, ecstatic and naked in the raw wounds of awakening. They are imbued with the fiery taste of the constantly disappearing sacred on the tongue. Mainly they are a call, as Walters says, to "forget everything you know and open."

— Eve Ensler, playwright, performer, feminist, activist, The Vagina Monologues; In the Body of the World; The Good Bod

In "Some Kiss We Want," Dorothy Walters effortlessly weaves mystical jewels from all the living traditions—Hinduism, Buddhism, Taoism, and the Abrahamic lineages— with succulent poetic language. The tapestry that emerges from the warp of wisdom with the weft of beauty is a magical carpet. Fly this book straight into the arms of the Beloved.

— Mirabai Starr, spiritual teacher, writer, mystic, The Interior Castle: St. Teresa of Avila; The Showings of Julian of Norwich; God of Love; Wild Mercy

The poetry of Dorothy Walters is rich with wisdom and heart and the wordsmith's skill, but most importantly it has presence. Each poem rings in the mind and works a strange alchemy in the soul, leaving us giddy and hungry for the secret contact of spirit and body. Some kiss indeed!

— Ivan Granger, editor, Poetry Chaikhana, Real Thirst, Poetry of the Spiritual Journey; The Longing In Between, Sacred Poetry from Around the World

Dorothy Walters has the heart and vision of a mystic and is rooted firmly in the ecstatic tradition, where the divine overflows into daily life. Her poems invite us into this holy mystery, kindling deep joy and love in her readers. Reading her poems becomes an act of prayer itself, inviting us to slow down and savor what is already within.

— Christine Valters Paintner, Ph.D, online Abbess of www.Abbeyof theArts.com and author of 7 books on spirituality and the arts

Dorothy Walters' poetry is inspired, arising from a deep immersion in her own awakened heart. Let her words resonate with your own heart.

— Sally Kempton, author, Meditation for the Love of It; Awakening Shakti

I think your poetry is beautiful and profound. The poems I have read are exquisite and to be treasured and they remind me strangely of Rumi.

— Anne Baring, The Dream of the Cosmos; The Mystic Vision; The Divine Feminine (with Andrew Harvey)

The ancient yogic texts tell us that poetry drips like ambrosia from the tongue of the yogi who has awakened Kundalini-Shakti – the divine feminine that rests within. They tell us that these sweet-as-honey words are a sign – a sign that you are in the presence of a true mystic. Read Dorothy Walters' words in this marvelous volume and you will have no doubt that you are in the presence of both an authentic mystic and a great poet.

— Teri Degler, author, The Divine Feminine Fire: Creativity and Your Yearning to Express Your Self

Dorothy Walters is the real thing because for her spiritual experience is primary, and her poetry (like a continuing fountain) comes out of that. She actually has something to say beyond the existential 'me' and the otherwise verbal complexity of poetry that has only 'words' to say. Like all true spiritual and mystical writers, her language is grounded in transparency and grace; and it resonates: her poems are a witness and a transmission. She's part of the perennial stream, and there her work will remain; refreshing weary travelers of all ages now and in the future. I salute her.

— Jay Ramsay, author, Kingdom of the Edge; Out of Time; Places of Truth; Monuments; Diamond Cutters

Crossing the border into the boundless domain of Source and returning is the epic journey of seekers on the quest for direct experience of the Infinite. Of those that truly make that journey, most are struck dumb by the magnificence of what lies beyond and how it reveals Itself to be fully present in every moment and everything. Fortunately for all who read her poetry, Dorothy Walters has been gifted with the rare ability to express in words the sounds and scents, the visions and insights, the feelings and the mind-obliterating Love that her encounters with the Infinite One have birthed in her body and soul. This fine collection of her poetry will call to the hearts and souls of all who read it and beckon them to read her other works in full!

— Lawrence Edwards, Ph.D, Founder and Director, Anam Cara Meditation Foundation; Author: Kali's Bazaar; Awakening Kundalini: The Path to Radical Freedom

SOME KISS WE WANT

(second edition)

Some Kiss We Want

POEMS SELECTED AND NEW

(second edition)

by Dorothy Walters

Introduction by Andrew Harvery

There is some kiss we want
with our whole lives,
the touch of Spirit on the body.
Seawater begs the pearl
to break its shell.
And the lily, how passionately
it needs some wild Darling!
At night, I open the window
and ask the moon to
come and press its face
into mine.
Breathe into me.
Close the language-door,
and open the love-window.
The moon won't use the door,
only the window.

RUMI
(tr. Coleman Barks)

SOME KISS WE WANT:
POEMS SELECTED AND NEW
Second Edition
by Dorothy Walters

Thanks to Coleman Barks and Harpers San Francisco for permission to use the title of the poem by the same name for the title of this book (Some Kiss We Want, from The Soul of Rumi). Thanks to Coleman Barks and Harpers San Francisco for permission to reprint the text of the poem entitled Some Kiss We Want from The Soul of Rumi.

ISBN-13: 978-0-9995658-7-2

Emergence Education Press
P.O. Box 63767, Philadelphia, PA 19147
www.EmergenceEducation.com

Cover photography and design by Silvia Rodrigues

For more information about Dorothy Walters visit:
www.DorothyWalters.com

Dedication

*This book is
dedicated to
Andrew Harvey,
beloved friend,
mentor,
and teacher,
from whom I
learned what it
means to be an
authentic mystic.*

ACKNOWLEDGMENTS

I also wish to thank the following individuals who offered unfailing support and inspiration during the many years during which these poems were created: Patricia Lay-Dorsey, Kathy Fowler, Karen Lester, Peggy Wrenn, Gail Thompson, Stephanie Marohn, Hélène des Rosiers and Jacqueline Arnold

INTRODUCTION

Of all modern visionary poets, Dorothy Walters is, to my mind, by far the wisest and most radiant. I was going to write "by far the best" and then checked myself: such triumphalism would betray the deepest of all Dorothy's qualities, both as a person and as a poet, her gently relentless humility forged from profound experience.

I would revere Dorothy's work even if I did not know her, even if she were not among the handful of people I love most in the world. Dorothy is now in her mid-nineties: to know her is to know someone who has been through a great deal in life, both deep sorrow and continuing revelation, who knows just how terrible is the situation we find ourselves in, but who has continued to explore in herself, and for all of us, sources of ever-deepening faith, resolve and joy. You could be forgiven for missing this heroic dimension to her work, pursued through years of steady devotion despite lack of wide recognition. Read these poems carefully, and tears of awe and gratitude will come to your eyes, and you will be forever subtly changed.

Andrew Harvey, author of Turn Me to Gold: 108 Poems of Kabir

Contents

Of Course 31

PART ONE

Marrow of Flame, Poems of the Spiritual Journey 33

Drowning in God. 35
Seekers 37
Smoke Clad 38
The Runaway 39
Don't Make Lists 40
At the Very Moment 41
More From The Tao 42
The Task. 43
The Entry 44
Nomads 45
A Golden Haze Or Halo. 46
Gifts 48
The Only Rule 49
Pain. 51
What The Prophets Said 52
What Is Happening. 53
The Woman Who Lived In A Cave 54
The Hermit Monk 57
Bodhidharma Returning 58
Persephone 60
The Witch 62
Her Body Revealed At Last 64
    1. Ice Plants 64
    1. Rainbows 64
    1. Before The Pleated Wings Of Summer 65
Scars of Rapture 66
The Yogi Inside. 68
Waiting 69
Teresa's Enigma 70
Locating The Invisible 71
When We Stumble And Find It. 72
The Other 73
The God Mother 74
    1. The Nurturer. 74

2. Our Lady Of The Plants And Animals. 74
3. Kali Goddess Of Death 75
The Woman Who Slept With Shiva. 77
God's Mistress 79
The Secret 80
A Hollow Throat 81
A Thousand Ways 83
Don't Turn Away 84
Love Flings Us Forward. 85
Oh, Yes 87

PART TWO

A Cloth Of Fine Gold, Poems of the Inner Journey. 89

A Cloth Of Fine Gold 91
Until Even The Angels 92
A Language You Once Knew. 93
Be Prepared To Swelter 94
Tasting The Light. 96
Taken 97
What Is It? 99
Carving Us Into Constant Love 100
A Hinge In Time 102
Brokeback Mountain 104
The Ascent. 105
And Even Then. 107
Still, I Am Shameless 108
Meditation. 110
Not A Thousand Prostrations 111
I Cannot Tell You. 114
What The Tulips Said 116
Kundalini Returning At The Seaside 117
The Truth About Chakras 119
Poem For Mary Oliver 120
An Angel Strayed Into Me 122
Mary Doty. 124
Rothko 126
Poems For Mirabai 127
1. The Besotted Follower 127
2. Only This 128
My Trident And Bell 129
Night After Night 130

More Love Poems To The Invisible. 131
This Gift. 131
Are You Willing! 133
Sufis 134
Your Ocean 138
Teresa In Ecstasy. 140
The Stages Of Bliss 141
What The Gods Require. 143
The Prophet 143
Finally We Took An Axe. 145
Like Flowers That Bloom At Midnight 146
Living With Buddha 148
I Will 155

PART THREE

The Ley Lines Of The Soul, Poems of Ecstasy and Ascension 157

Ley Lines 159
Before. 160
Who You Are. 161
How To See An Angel. 163
Whatever You Offer 166
The Seeker Attempts To Return 167
Whatever You Do. 169
The Mystery 171
Bethrothed. 172
What I Can Tell You 174
Nobody Understands This 175
The Surprise. 176
Love Poems For The Invisible 177
    Out Of Nowhere 177
    For So Many Years 177
    Like A Mongolian. 178
    This Love 178
    The Beckoning 180
    What? 181
Still More Love Poems For The Invisible 182
    1. What I Have Given You 182
    2. Only The Lovemaking 182
    3. Whatever You Do. 183
Particles Dancing. 184
Hymn To The Nameless One 185

The Ley Lines Of The Soul 187
Even If You Have Trudged. 188
In A Strange Tongue 190
After 191
St. Teresa Reflects On Her Raptures 192
Everything Moving. 194
A Silk To Course Fiber 195
If You Want 197
The Lives Of The Soul 198
The Awakening. 199
Dancing With The Great Lion 201
Going Beyond 202

PART FOUR

Penelope's Loom, Poems of Turning Matter into Spirit. 205

Penelope's Loom 206
This Bead Of Light 208
The God Particle 209
Ever Arriving 211
Theories. 212
Who We Are 215
The Cave Painters Of Lascaux 217
The Photographer 219
Beethoven The Immeasurable 220
"My Job Is Turning Matter Into Spirit" 221
The Renegade Poet Confesses 222
Sea Change 224
Persephone Again 225
The Under Water Poems 227
    1. The Frond 227
    2. What The Fish Said 227
    3. What The Empty Shell Said 228
Belgian Lace 230
White Heron Becoming Sky 232
The Climber 234
Where Shadows Speak 237
The Black Swan 239
Toward Bethlehem 240
The Beings Within 242
    The Warrior 242
    The Skeptic. 242

The Coward 243
The Child 244
The Lost Adult 244
The Saint. 245
The Awakened One Leaves 246
On My Eightieth Birthday. 247
On Your Slender body 248
The Celebrity Lover 250
If Your Heart. 252
It Is Time 253
Things To Be Emptied 254

PART FIVE

From Unmaskign The Rose, A Record of a Kundalini Initiation 255

The Supplicants 256
A Golden Haze Or Halo. 257
Preparing To Greet The Goddess 259
Meeting With Silence. 260
Who Move Among Us 261
Ruined By Your Beauty 262
Listening To Music In Poses. 263
This Music Of Light 264
Love Takes Us Into Its Holy Ground 265
Rishis 266

PART SIX

New Poems 267

Start With Roses 268
Signs In The Sky 269
Before Galileo 270
The Moment Which Changes Everything. 272
What Will You Do 274
On This Music 276
Who Went Unheard 277
Scarlet Berries 279
For Michael Black, Again 281

Our Time 283

Lalita 285

Only If Shiva 286

Maybe Somewhere 287

The Buddha Within 288

Tibetan, Resonant 289

How It Is 290

One Of The Ways 291

Flooding And Blind 292

Who She Is 293

Now That You Have Destroyed Me 295

When She Came 297

For So Very Long 298

Rough Bark 299

These Words 300

Fool's Gold 301

The Winemakers 302

After That 303

Your Body 304

The Offering 305

Is It The Night Of Becoming? 307

Zen Poem 309

After Kabir 310

Krishna To Arjuna 312

Listening 313

Orpheus 314

The Skeptics 315

Dancing Gods 316

Prayer On A Day Of Bliss 317

I Became The Fish 318

Stages 319

How It Will Be 320

Her Dark Face 321

She 322

Journeys 323

Appendix 324

Author's Note 332

PREFACE

In 1981, I experienced sudden, spontaneous Kundalini awakening. This was not a one-time experience. It was a reality that immediately transformed and then governed my life for the next thirty some years, right up to and including the present moment.

Kundalini, though now more present in the consciousness of the Western audience, is still a seriously misunderstood phenomenon. It is looked upon by many as a mysterious and indeed esoteric force, something that the ordinary citizen will never experience even when it is sought through practice and discipline. It is often (mistakenly) associated with extreme sexual arousal or a time of uncontrolled jerking and flailing of the limbs as a release of nervous energy takes place.

Neither of these states characterizes my journey.

For me and many others blessed with such awakening (and I believe the numbers are increasing exponentially) it is a sacred revelation, one destined ultimately to lead to greater intimacy with divine reality, if not full enlightenment, as well as universal transformation of our universe.

Kundalini offers times of joy and ecstasy as well as pain and a certain amount of discomfort as the various "bodies" (physical, spiritual, emotional, and mental) are cleared to allow for a smoother energetic flow through the system. However, each seemingly unsought new state of consciousness is a part of an ongoing process, leading to full transformation of the many attributes of the aspirant.

My awakening occurred in Kansas in 1981, when Kundalini was still essentially unknown in most of the West and certainly unacknowledged in my part of the world. There were no gurus in my vicinity to help or guide me so I forged ahead on my own, telling virtually no one of the mysterious process to which I had now surrendered, one I considered a profoundly sacred alchemy. I did keep a journal of the constantly changing phases of this unfolding, and this journal became the basis of *Unmasking the Rose, A Record of a Kundalini Initiation*. It was indeed an initiatory experience, an introduction into ways of being and perceiving the world around me unlike any I had known or experienced before. I was now a "new person," visited daily by a guiding "inner guru" that I could not see or even name, but which drew me ever closer to Source, the invisible center of boundless love in a kind of "marriage of the soul."

Among other new experiences, I now underwent repeated episodes of spiritual bliss, a bodily ecstasy akin to the "raptures" that St. Teresa of Avila described many centuries ago, as well as intermittent episodes of pain as the body attempted to adjust to these new energies. Such experience was completely new to me, and I basically had no one to explain to me what was happening—I somehow trusted the "guide within" and told almost no one, though I did, as I say, keep a journal of this mysterious process. I kept my secret locked inside until—some fifteen years later—I met Andrew Harvey in San Francisco, where he was teaching. He generously heard my story and encouraged me to write about my experience in Unmasking the Rose as well as in poems reflecting the stages of this spiritual rebirth.

And I did.

The result was several books of mystical poetry, and it is the best contents of these volumes (plus several newer poems) that are now offered as Some Kiss We Want: Poems Selected and New. Each poem is an attempt to capture the ineffable in words, to reveal the inner truth of spiritual transformation and show Spirit at work in a most intimate way in the psyche of the human subject.

Spiritual reshaping does not follow a straight-line chronology. Bliss alternates with pain, and ecstasy is often followed by grief. These poems attempt to capture such moments, giving each its due in the constant progression to ever-higher states of consciousness. Ultimately, after many years, what begins as spiritual passion often ends in stillness and inner calm.

Like Gopi Krishna, I believe that Kundalini (under whatever name or guise) is a primary engine of the transformation of consciousness that the world is now undergoing. These transfigurations point to the mostly unfamiliar stages that many of us are entering as we move into a new evolutionary plane, one inevitable for human kind as we throw off old forms and systems and fashion the world anew into a more sacred and benevolent design.

It is my hope that these verses will inspire others on a similar path of inner transformation, and tell them that they are not alone in their journey, but that they are part of a larger collective shift as the Beloved enters and sustains what some have called "the divinization of matter" in its human manifestation.

For me, my earlier awakening has provided constant hope for the future of our species, for, considering the conditions and time in which this remarkable event occurred, I must conclude that indeed anything is possible anywhere, once Spirit enters and shapes the process.

(Note: Andrew Harvey's account of my awakening experience, originally written as an introduction to Marrow of Flame, is included in the appendix to this volume, for those not familiar with my story.)

Dorothy Walters

Boulder, Colorado, 2019

OF COURSE

There is some kiss we want
with our whole lives,
the touch of Spirit on the body.

— Rumi

Yes, of course,
that is the thing we want,
touch of Spirit
on body,
delight of soul
enfleshed and opened,
trembling at last,
how could we not
remember how
it was before,
when You were not there,
when all we had
was this cloud of longing
and did not even know
what it was
we were looking for?

— Dorothy Walters

PART I

Marrow Of Flame

POEMS OF THE SPIRITUAL JOURNEY

2000

DROWNING IN GOD

Those drowned in God want to be more drowned.
— ***Rumi***

Everything in.
Nothing held back,
not the bewildered face in the mirror,
the memory of the first time,
the quarrel and reconciliation.

This wind will sweep you
from yourself
the way clouds
absorb an ocean,
the way fire seeks out
the marrow of flame.

When it is over
you will be less than a bit
of twisted weed,
smaller than a splinter
of sea-blackened wood.

You will not miss
your lost possessions
nor even remember their uses.
When someone shows you
your cast items,
your familiar appendages
and agendas,

even your flashing ornaments,
you will look puzzled,
and ask, What are these?
Their functions or relevance?
I have drunk from a deep well.
What are these sips you offer,
"just for the taste?"
I'm looking for a world
sky deep in water.

SEEKERS

Each of us is searching for
a wise man or woman
to lead us,
to present us
a scroll heavy with answers.

Some of us have climbed the mountain,
tracked the glacier's crust,
lain down in snow for days, years,
burning away to essence,
preparing.

Others have clung
to the underside of overhanging rock
until their fingers turned
to stone,
until they were riveted
like lead
to this thin edge of certainty.

And others wander, drifting like mist
through the valleys.

What is it we are seeking?
What will we do if we are brushed
by this lion's mane?

SMOKE CLAD

Only the stunned and bewildered ever glimpse the throne.
— Rumi

All of us have been stunned enough,
and bewildered enough,
passing again and again over landscape
we could never name—
sun where stars should be,
moon coming forth at noon—
ourselves leaping through exploding
rainbows of flame,
landing, perhaps, at the heart,
the silent core,
hands glowing and empty,
bodies clothed only in ashes and tint.

THE RUNAWAY

The Place where you are right now
God circled on a map for you.
— Hafiz

The poet says
God has put a circle around you on a map
to locate you in sacred space.
Then why do you keep tunneling
underground,
carving labyrinths for your escape?

DON'T MAKE LISTS

Every day a new flower rises
from your body's fresh soil.
Don't go around looking
for fallen petals
in a fairy tale when you've
got the golden plant
right here, now,
shooting forth in light from your eyes,
your awakening crown.

Don't make lists, or explore ancient accounts.
Forget everything you know
and open.

AT THE VERY MOMENT

No matter what you know,
someone is always
wanting to correct you,
to sell you a bill of goods
from the shop marked
"authority."
All the "authorities" got
frozen into stone years
ago after the great flood
wiped out original knowledge
and left behind only these granite shadows.

Reality is
always soft clay,
ever shifting and changing
its shape.

Fire it into form
and
at the very moment
you are hailing it as
final truth
it will break in your hands.

MORE FROM THE TAO

1.

When some put on robes
and others bow down before them,
it is already lost.

2.

When some speak endlessly,
while others sit wide-mouthed
writing in notebooks,
it is not present.

3.

When groups begin
to look all alike,
and comb their hair the same way
and can be found doing identical things
at a certain hour,
nothing is happening.

THE TASK

This is like a lover
who gives no rest,
but demands, and demands, and demands.

Do you think this is a time for pausing,
for lying about under the pine trees,
sampling your lunch pail?

If you are chosen to be the consort,
do not refuse the King.
If you have been outfitted
for a journey to the Himalayas,
do not nibble away your provisions
before you reach the ice.

THE ENTRY
(homage to Kabir)

Not from saying names,
or praying to statuary.
Not from holding your breath
till you are blue in the face.
Not from twisting your torso this way, now that,
till you are like a string
striving to become a knot.
Not from reading saints' lives
or fingering a billion beads.

Only this:

The moment between the breaths.
The stillness between the notes.
A firefly extinguishes itself,
bleeds darkness
before its final flare.

NOMADS

Beyond this flame-desert, other, even wilder deserts.
— Rumi

Here, where we have traced
sand circles by day,
danced ourselves to lostness
beneath the night's pale eye,
till we fall in a love trance
on the seething, swimming floor,
you say—other deserts,
more flaming, more wild?
So, then, when we can no longer stand,
we can always make our way
on hands and gold-laced knees,
we can always find a way
to swim through tossing sand.

A GOLDEN HAZE OR HALO

I know you are there, waiting to find me,
to take me in your heavy jaws,
to gulp me like a morsel
or cough me up like
a briar.

For I am covered in thorns.
No, that's not so.
I am slicked over, oiled,
like something disguised
for a celebration.
I have made myself
an easy prey,
something to be quickly swallowed
and digested
or else spat out in disgust.

You keep calling,
I keep looking the other way.
I beg my responsibilities,
my serious obligations.
You hear none of my
protestations—
they are irrelevant, weightless as air.

You sit back on your great haunches,
swish your tail,

make a warning growl in your throat.
I no longer remember how long
you have been there,
when you came.
Each time I scanned the landscape,
you are always what I saw.
Your mane floats like a golden haze or halo
around your unfathomable face.
Now you are pacing again.

GIFTS

The Divine Lover, says Hafiz,
will smash your windows out
to throw in holy gifts.

Did you realize
that the windows would be
all the openings into your own body,
each pore,
that your very soul
would crumble,
that you would lie awake nights
listening to your bones cry
out like hungry ghosts grieving
their lost worlds?

THE ONLY RULE

Longing is the core of mystery.
Longing itself brings the cure.
The only rule is, "Suffer the pain."
— Rumi

How could this happen again?
To me, of all people,
the one who knows,
who has been through
the gold-tongued flame
so many times
that even the edges of
her shadow
are singed to
a deeper blue.

How could it come about
that I, of all the rest,
the one wandering and lost
for so many lives
of suffering,
must stand upright
for yet another slaying?

How could I not remember?

Why would I venture in
to stroll the avenues
of the deserted city,
forgetting the blade's
delicate thrust,
heedless quiver of love?

Do I not have scars
to prove my foolhardiness?
And now what prize
am I seeking?
More scars,
more sacred wounds
to savor once again
this secret baptism of pain?

PAIN

We bury our pain in a secret crypt,
stealing out at night to worship or pray.

We insist our pain is nameless,
and therefore does not exist.

We hide our pain behind the crockery
on a high shelf,
convinced that when we take it down
it will be less vibrant,
muted by dust and silken webs.

We put it in with the silver
which we use only on Rare Occasions,
removing it with the flatware now and again,
to polish and make inventory.

We wear our pain inside
a small locket around our neck.
We carry it as a stone hidden in our shoe,
or else as a thorn riding our flank.

We fasten a red ribbon around our throat,
so that we do not speak or whisper.

WHAT THE PROPHETS SAID

They said that the planet would vibrate
at an ever increasing rate.
They said there would be more heat,
more shaking, everywhere.
That many mountains and beings would be torn
open,
and the spilling oceans would devour the land.
That time itself would accelerate,
until it arrived at absolute zero,
conjunction then of no time, no space,
merely the terror of the real.

WHAT IS HAPPENING

Moment to moment
we ask, what is happening?
The sound of shattering everywhere,
is it the world, fragmenting at last,
or our own hearts cracking,
the final break-up of ice?

It was cold there.
At night
the stars came out
and looked down on me—
my quiet austerity,
my meek accommodations—
with a cool camaraderie,
ice acknowledging ice.

My meditations were my passion,
the gods in their attributes,
their colors and forms.
Each had its fixed aspects,
demanding perfect recall.
I labored, hour after hour,
year melting into year.
To err would risk
sacrilege, shame before
heaven.
But the figures grew always sharper,
my discernment more refined
till the images breathed with life
and I and they were one.

For comfort, I had my small
butter lamp and the candle,
but of course I saved these for

only the essential.

Mostly the dying sun
signaled the end
of my day.
Again, I rose
when the light
flooded the valley below
with filtered honey,
touched the tip
of my sleeping box
with its prodding finger.

I had nowhere
to lie down properly.
The box was not
long enough to lie in,
nor wide enough to stretch.
I did not mind.
My aim was not to be
comfortable,
but to be still,
and enter the silence.

The only voices I heard
were the crying of those
mountain birds,
the wind cracking against
the boulders,
the rain slashing at

the cliff.

But this was what I had
dreamed of,
the life I had come to live.
This was the person I had chosen to be.
How could I flee my dharma?
Besides, I had done it
so many times before
it was easy,
a familiar pattern,
like a garment one folds
and unfolds,
moonlight,
darkness.

Tenzin Palmo, who was born in East London, became one of the first
Westerners to be ordained as a Tibetan Buddhist nun (1964). For twelve
years, she lived in a cave in the Himalayas, seeking Full Awakening. See Cave
in the Snow by Vicki Mackenzie.

THE HERMIT MONK

Because I was nothing
within my coarse shirt,
I found everything without.

Snail path stirring,
blood slash of cardinal rising,
water-stained rocks with holy faces
all entered me.

My flesh became a translucent veil,
admitting all freshness.
My bones were wavering
pillars set in a house of light.

When they found me sunk in my leafbed,
my hair was moss
feathering the tree roots,
my hand a shellcup
holding water,
and flowers burnt in my eyes.

BODHIDHARMA RETURNING

(Around 527 A. D., Bodhidharma carried the message of Buddhism from
India into China, where it developed as Ch'an [known later as Zen in
Japan.] The speaker, in a curious dream, saw herself as a highly diminished
reincarnation of the ancient patriarch.)

I once carried a world on my back
into a new land.
The emperor, affronted,
challenged me,
but I turned my face away,
and did not respond
for many years.
At last he acknowledged my presence,
and the people, seeing,
became my flock.

My fame and wisdom spread
till everyone knew my name,
the strange practice I brought with me
now accepted as a familiar household rite.
My work finished, I withdrew
into the back pages of history,
someone who once did something
of significance.

After I died, I waited several centuries
then felt the world trembling for my return.

I came down,
shrunken to a seed
cast haphazardly on unfamiliar soil.
Somehow my intensity had waned,
so that there was never a real blossoming,
a passionate avowal,
only darkness, a constant pressing
against unyielding earth,
a soft battering upward
through the tangled roots,
and silence stretching,
stretching,
toward the thin filament
of sun.

PERSEPHONE

You may think this is a story
about a woman going down to a man,
her lover, sinking like smoke
into his flesh,
dissolving like
mist into the
shrubbery.

I tell you, her descent
was not to alien ground,
but rather a spiral through herself,
mysteries yielding at every turn.

Oh, he was useful to her,
offering as he did
instruction in her own
forgotten rites,
leading her, as he could,
to rediscoveries
of what she had always known.

He thought himself a mentor.
Actually, for her he was
like someone figuring
in a dream,
someone
occasional and
indistinct, whose

significance
was never clear.

And when, called back,
summoned by Lady Mother,
she rose, clutching in her hand something—
a seed, a flower.
She flew upward
like a figure from Chagall
to where that woman waited,
mirror image coming clear,
already forgetting what it was
she left abandoned all below.

THE WITCH

I was always a nice girl
with a few bad habits.
I whistled a lot
out gathering eggs.
When my brothers hand-wrestled
I insisted on winning.
The villagers said
I walked like a boy.

My father used to eye me from afar,
and hold private conversations
in the corner with mother.

When the other girls married
I took no notice,
though I threw rice at the church door
along with the rest.
Whatever I was seeking
it wasn't this:
a screaming cradle
and a man with soot for fingers.

Once I went to a gathering
in the heart of the forest
where shadows make shadows
I learned my true name.

Since then I have lived here
at the edge of the woods
with my tabby and my charms,
my thatch needing repair.
My potions are famous
all over these parts.
When people come seeking
from near and from far,
they ask what goes in.
I mutter, *Roots and berries.*
Berries and roots.
How can I tell them
it is themselves they taste?

HER BODY REVEALED AT LAST

Nature is Him, my friend,
One Dance, one Body.
— Rumi

1. ICE PLANTS

I can say nothing
of the lost kingdoms—
Atlantis, Shambhala—
the mystic crossing lines.
But here,
these trembling spears of sun,
swimming mirrors of russet and green,
transparent fish blades thrusting,
dancing upwards in this net of light:
the ocean's luminous catch,
ready for tomorrow's market,
ready to be tasted,
to be swallowed whole.

2. RAINBOWS

As if the storm were not enough,
then there were rainbows.
Rainbows, not made of sky,
but fashioned from the waves' own sheen,
hued ribbons unfurling—
lilac, amber, blue—

flinging themselves across the line of spray
in arcs that streamed along the spume
like world horizons blown to color,
like energies of water sprites
released in shooting circling bands
in some celebration we witnessed silently,
not knowing then
what it was we were looking on,
or if we were meant to see.

3. BEFORE THE PLEATED WINGS OF SUMMER

Nothing is wild here,
but they push through
in ways to deceive
all but the keenest eye.
As if seed randomly sown
ascended in throats
of color—
great swatches of iris
singing darkly
along with the
spills of poppy,
dust of saffron and gold,
white daisy grazing the beds—
I think she is leaping forth again
in her gauzy muslin,
rehearsing her coy fandango,
her spriggy green gavot.

SCARS OF RAPTURE

Shams, I have done everything I know
so this would not happen.

You came into my life
like a wing of fire,
possessing and
possessed by something
not seen.

When you first spoke,
my books turned to clay a
nd my throat closed
around a lost syllable.

Your eyes burned over me,
leaving scars of rapture,
my spirit became a field
swept clean by flame.

Can you think how it was
that morning I woke first,
and found you,
an unbound mystery,
by my side.

Or the day we did not eat,
but drank from one another's light
till we were ribboned by dusk.

The air here holds only emptiness,
a little dust stirring.
I think there will be wind tonight,
and the camels will cry out
in their sleep.

(When Rumi's beloved teacher Shams mysteriously disappeared,
Rumi was inconsolable. He never fully recovered from the loss.)

THE YOGI INSIDE

What she wants
is not words nor fastenings,
nor doctrine spilling over her
like salt,
nor precincts set off by markers.
This is sacred space.

Wherever she steps is holy ground.
Moving, she traces streams of light
with her hands, her body.
When she listens,
she becomes a spreading tree of silence
that knows only itself.

WAITING

The jeweled cloud sways overhead,
waiting.
Meanwhile, our cells are turning to air,
finer and finer arrangements of light.

TERESA'S ENIGMA

How can I explain this?
Yesterday, pain cleaving a path
over shoulder and arm,
eyes stunned by arrows of light,
back a maze of burning rivers.

Today, Vivaldi, Stabat
Mater, a subtle lifting in the
heart, wrists floating in
rapture,
in my mouth the taste of honey and flame.

Like the speaker in the poem, St. Teresa of Avila experienced periods of
intense pain and suffering as well as transcendent rapture during her
transformation. Such extreme oscillations between pleasure and pain are
often a characteristic of those undergoing awakening of the Kundalini
energies, a highly charged spiritual phenomenon becoming more and more
frequent in today's world.

LOCATING THE INVISIBLE

I have nothing to go on,
not even a name.
If asked, what tradition?
I can only look away.

Is it enough,
this touching within,
this constant infusion of "the other"?

WHEN WE STUMBLE AND FIND IT

We all have our favorite themes,
the ones we say over and over
in a thousand different tongues.

Mine is the moment which
changed my life
forever.
Not the one I planned for
or expected, but the one which simply
happened.
It could have been a
revelation
speaking from a cloud of fire.
It could have been
a rare accomplishment, election
descending like a dove after
so many years.

It was none of these.
Merely a moment,
the one I keep returning to,
feeling along the wall for the
hidden latch
which will spring open
and reveal the undefined.

THE OTHER

I can stand it
that you arrive with no name,
come in without face or form .

I can bear the reality
of pressure without weight,
movement without
presence.

But how do you choose your time
to appear,
the moment to go?
What is it you keep almost saying?
And where are you
when you are not here,
with me?

THE GOD MOTHER

1. THE NURTURER

She is a breast
hanging down from the sky:
open your mouth
and feel the
thin sweet milk
of the sun
roll down your throat.

2. OUR LADY OF THE PLANTS AND ANIMALS

Everything blooms
from her body:
her arms are long-stemmed lilies,
her ears the shells
from which the anemones spring,
purple hyacinths spiral
between her thighs.

Small creatures
unfold from her
sides and belly:
rabbit, ground squirrel, pig,
the cautious field mouse
and the cat
who will eat it,

the fish
and the larger fish
swimming forth together.
From her throat
five thrushes
are leaving
in eddies of sound.

2. KALI, GODDESS OF DEATH

She wears her corded
necklace of skulls a
nd her arms hold
many strong implements,
one is silver
dipped in red—
we have forgotten its name but
we know its meaning:
one sweep
and
everything vanishes,
we, our fleshly forms
and intentions,
our notions of things,
dissolving,
one swift stroke
and the pattern of millennia is reversed,
atoms shattered back
to nothingness,

worlds tumbling
back to darkness,
to before.

THE WOMAN WHO SLEPT WITH SHIVA

I called him down,
and when he came
I opened my arms
as if to a lost husband, or child.

I thought I would turn to ash
in that brilliant flame,
my body, lustrous
as a crystal,
surrendering its defining atoms of gold,
its threads of memory, even,
to that blinding dance.

Everything
dissolved into a
wave of feeling till
nothing was left
but the essential light.

Then I came back.
I slipped away
to the scullery,
and my bed at the top
of the attic stairs
where I keep my amulet
and my bracelet of stone.

At first I stayed silent,
thinking of what it might mean.
Now I am telling my story,
but no one wishes to hear.
They say they must tend to the weaving,
the harvest ready to come in.
They worry about sons
who complain of the brides they have chosen,
about daughters who scorch the rice
and forget to put salt in the soup.
They think that the heat has gotten to me,
recall that my mother's father
was always a bit strange.
I think I have been
on an improbable adventure;
at night I dream of a face
I can't quite see,
although I almost glimpse it, at times,
in the pitcher I carry
from the stream at morning,
in the violet clouds
that gather at dusk.

GOD'S MISTRESS

The other bears
his ring and name.

I lurk in doorways,
clothed in shadow,
waiting for a touch
so intense
I no longer care
what they call me,
or whisper about in the kitchens.

I am the wanton who keeps close company
with what the fathers denounce
and the many shun.
When God comes calling on
his whore,
the sidewalks empty,
and all curtains close.

THE SECRET

I carry it around
like a flower,
or a flame
concealed under a dark canister,
its glass so thick
no light can pierce
its black skin.

Sometimes I think
I am no better
than some Caliban
raving in his cave,
conjuring visions,
or an ordinary housewife,
who plays harlot
by night.

Sometimes I think I
grow tired of my burden,
want to set it down:
let someone else bear this cargo of love.

A HOLLOW THROAT
(for Helen)

Jalalludin, what have you done to me?
I have given you everything,
but nothing has prepared me
for this.
First, you took my jewels,
my jade ankle bracelets,
my sapphire bands,
leaving behind only a tracing of light
to mark where they had been.
Then my veils dropped, one by one,
in a sweep of silk.
How could I protect this
nothingness I had become,
this crystal abyss.

Before, when you came you wore
a vague plume or turban
making you seem real,
a being more like me,
or else, invisible, you
opened the hidden passages
by silence or breath,
or a movement like flowers
swaying under water;
even then the secret bliss waves
were partly mine

and I knew who I was

Now, everything has dissolved to music,
a single note from a struck Tibetan bowl,
like a hollow throat gathering the world
into itself.
Even this I could have borne.
But there was no instrument or bell,
only a single pure tone rising through
this woman before me,
universe beginning,
lost primordial hum,
and I—as no one—was entered, sounded,
as a current moved through my body
like God.

A THOUSAND WAYS

The Beloved knows a thousand ways
to enter your body.

When you were young,
she sent you a lover of flesh
who stood near
to awaken your nature.

Now God is your unseen paramour
arriving without notice
on unexpected occasions.
To discover her,
turn gently, and follow your breath
to the center of your being.

DON'T TURN AWAY

Don't turn away.
I know,
I am no longer the young dancer.
I sit quietly, hands folded, a stiff back.
But even now, break the channels open.
Let it come in,
that something which tells me who you are.
I want to be bathed in it,
a hundred rose gardens opening at once.
Even if it is only
a quiver of feeling,
let it happen.
Tell me you are there.

LOVE FLINGS US FORWARD

Yes, of course.

What good is it,
this feeling,
this ecstasy
surging in the
limbs, the
heart,
abyss of bliss
which swallows you each
day, stunning consciousness,
silencing the tongue.

What purpose has been served
if the war, cancer,
oblivious parent or callous mate
with a blow or an unlucky turn of things
shatters the dream
which is your life,
weaving a dark stain
over your gleaming spirit garb.

The inscrutable
advances, whirls us like milky spores
over the rocks of the stream,
force echoing force,
life embracing life,

dashing us along
as if nothing mattered
but this, the hammering wave,
its forward rush,
this riot of love
across the weathering stone.

OH, YES

I wanted to make love until
we were dust and ashes.
Li-Po

That's it.
Dust and ashes,
and a flame in which we burn
always,
a crescent blaze of love,
surfaces dissolving,
until nothing is left of us
but a fine ash
at the core
and then that, too, melting
to a nothingness, only a marker
where a somebody, a something, once was.

PART 2

A Cloth Of Fine Gold

POEMS OF THE INNER JOURNEY

2008

A CLOTH OF FINE GOLD

You may think
that first lit flame
was the ultimate blaze,
the holy fire revealed.

What do you know
of furnaces?
This is a sun that returns
again and again, refining,
igniting,
pouring your spirit
through a cloth of delicate gold
until all dross is taken
and you are sweet as
clarified butter
in god/the goddess' mouth.

What the heart wants
is to follow its true passion,
to lie down with it
near the reeds beside
the river,
to devour it in the caves
between the desert dunes,
to sing its notes
into the morning sky
until even the angels
wake up
and take notice
and look around
for their beloved.

A LANGUAGE YOU ONCE KNEW

There will be an invitation.
It will not come tied in ribbons
nor a message streaming down
from the sky.

There will be no Roman candles
sizzling
nor brilliant colors
exploding overhead.

Instead there will be a soft
whisper
in your ear,
something in a language
you once knew
and are trying to learn again.

In order to hear it,
you will need to
put down all your packages,
stop everything you are doing
and stand very still
and wait. . .
until something stirs inside.

If you want to go there,
check your boots and your
water bottle carefully.
Find the map
that the old one gave you
so long ago
and do your best to
follow it,
though often
you will make the wrong turn,
go astray.

Be prepared to swelter
under many suns,
drown
in countless rivers.

You will be shipwrecked many times,
or else burnt to cinder,
dust to dust.

You will meet strange winged creatures
who have no names,
beings descending
from the sky
or rising up like cloud specters
from below.

They will tell you
how to continue,
what paths to follow,
but check carefully
what they say.

Sometimes you will
fall into caverns or
caves, and will not
know
how to get out
until you see a
faint light coming
from a crack or crevice,
lit wings beckoning.

When you at last arrive,
you may not remember
who you are,
what you were seeking,
why you came.

It will not matter.

Now only silence will do.

TASTING THE LIGHT

It will arrive suddenly,
when you are unaware.

It will come over you swiftly,
lightning flash
across a large surface of stone.

After everything has melted,
there will be the taste
of bronze and honeyed fruit,
burnt cinnamon,
something blue and electric in the air.

TAKEN

First, you must let your heart
be broken open
in a way you have never
felt before, cannot imagine.

You will
not know if what you are feeling
is anguish or joy,
something predestined
or merely old wounds
flowing once more,
reminders of all that is
unfinished in your life.

Something will flood into
your chest
like air sweetened by
desert honeysuckle,
love that is too strong.

You will stand there,
very still,
not seeing what this is.
Later, you will not remember
any of this
until the next time
when you will say,

yes, yes, I have known this
before, it has come again,
just as your lids close shut
again.

WHAT IS IT?

Not a sexual explosion
rocking the flesh.

Nor a spasm of longing
triggering the blood.

More like perfume s
uffusing a room
filled with daffodils.

Or the barely heard sound
of a distant wind chime
resonating all your bones
to bliss.

Do you know how many times
I have opened my body to Yours,
how often I have become
whatever it is You are.

I never know just when
You will arrive,
how You are going to look
that day.

Sometimes you are
Shiva, tendrils flaming
ever dancing to keep the world alive.

Sometimes that Buddha
who lives in my front room,
wise master,
vessel of compassion,
container of sensuous joy.

Yesterday You were
just an image
on a temple wall,
some long vanished holy man or woman
with an inviting smile,
no one I had heard of
before.

The form does not matter,
only that you have come
once more.

A HINGE IN TIME

And then there was the pain,
so vast it was like
a hinge in time,
an antediluvian landscape
where memories burned the breath
of all that moved,
scalded the restless hours,
kept us quivering
and still.

There were no recipes
or ancient nostrums to heal, potions
or sages to dispense counsel,
our agony kept us burrowing
ever deeper
into the crevasses of our soul
seeking answers
that
did not come.
Until at last we
made
final surrender,
leapt into the abyss
of waiting
darkness,
gave up trying to know or fathom
with our riddled minds,
relinquished everything,

even the last scattered particles
of who we were.
And then the sweetness
moved again.

BROKEBACK MOUNTAIN

(Brokeback Mountain is the name of a movie which played in 2006. It tells the story of two lovers, male cowboys, who fell in love one summer and later were separated through the condemnations of a rejecting society.)

I keep telling myself
it was only a movie,
but no,
that grief has taken over my soul,
moved in like a thief
and now inhabits
the whole house,
this house with dark ribbons
on the door.

Old wounds throbbing once again,
old sorrows weeping
like statues in a burial ground.

They came together
like two lightning clouds
clashing, touched by a rod,
a brief flash sweeping across
the granite stones.
Momentary roar
of thunder,
the beast springing . . .
Then silence
everywhere.

THE ASCENT

Yes, there is a mountain.

Yes, you are on it,
struggling upward, s
tumbling over boulder
and rock.

There are others climbing with you.
Sometimes you nod
to one another,
sometimes you move in silence.

Occasionally, the clouds break open,
reveal a hazy glory up ahead,
something green and golden,
fairy tale kingdom from a child's
picture book.

Meanwhile, heavy legs lifting
again and again,
stone upon stone layering
the rising trail.
You think there must be an easier way,
a shortcut or secret tunnel.
Someone will
surely come for
you.

But if you imagine you are, one day,
going to be lifted up by an angel
and whisked to the top once more,
and there be fitted with shining golden wings
to carry you to unseen Edens yet beyond,
no, that will not happen.

Your path is here,
plodding over hard rubble
and scree
in a light that is failing,
an atmosphere that
ever thins.

Sometimes you're not sure
there is a mountain.
If you are there, moving upward,
toward some intended destination,
some longed for journey's end.

AND EVEN THEN

And if, say, one day
you reach the summit of the holy mount
and are there shattered utterly by light,
even then,
you must go on
not like a saint spiraling upward,
delicate feet barely tracing
invisible arcs of air,
but back once more
at the granite foot,
the rubbled start of it all
where you join again the struggling band,
pilgrims climbing together
on hands and rock-torn knees.

Who am I
to say things about Love?

Even on days like today
when memory alone
must suffice...

Sometimes it is enough
just to think
of all that has happened
between us,
midnight
meetings in broad
daylight, love
strokes
from invisible hands.

I no longer grieve
for the lost embrace,
but wait for the
certain return,
the knock at the window
sure to come.

Still, I am shameless
in my need,
like an aging mistress
who fingers old ribbons

and pearls
for reassurance.

Even God has moments of longing.

MEDITATION

I am not a Buddhist
nor am I a yogi.

My robe has no
special emblem
or design.

My Great Teacher
is Silence.

I sit here now,
listening.

NOT A THOUSAND PROSTRATIONS
(Inspired by Mary Oliver)

1.
You do not have to
change your name
in order for God
to love you.

You are not required to rise
at a certain hour
nor wear a robe
of a prescribed color
because that's what
the others have chosen to do.

You needn't make
the thousand prostrations
nor circumnavigate the holy mountain
a hundred times
nor dwell on an image
of an imaginary form
until you think
that being is who you are.

But you must wash your heart again and again
in the pure fountain where sanctity dwells.

You must cleanse your spirit many times over
in the cauldrons of love.

Only love, my friend,
can take you there.
Only the fiercest seekers
find the way.

2.
Still no one requires
that you be perfect,
that you turn away from the world
and live in a dark cavern
like a saint preparing to ascend.
Or that you stripe your back
with lashes, expiation
for the world's gross blunders,
your own hidden
miscalculations.

It isn't even necessary
to be fully informed,
to know all about everything,
or even a single thing,
for that matter.

What is important
is to be who you are,
to come ahead
with your small allotment of wisdom

garnered through the years, or face
your residue of compassion
eager to be shared.

If you paused to feed the pigeons
in the park one day,
that will count for you.
If you saw what was happening
to the forest
or spoke out against the sullying
of the noble sea,
heard the cry of the children
or the rising drums of war
and raised your voice in protest,
that will suffice.

Meanwhile,
dance as naked as you can.
Breathe your secret breath.
Let the world's warm currents
enter your body,
show you the way.

I do not know
if God
is a thing
or a process,
or a being
or a presence.

I cannot tell you
how the world
was constructed,
or when it began
or by whom.

I cannot unravel
the tables of meaning,
the diagrams
and the scales of comparison,
the charts and the long explanations
of everything
that has ever been.

What I know is this:
this moment,
this kiss,
this infinite longing,
endless loving and being loved
by one

who has no name
in a place
that does not exist.

WHAT THE TULIPS SAID
(inspired by Louise Gluck)

Down here
where darkness
thickens
in this tight sleeve of earth,
and filaments of root
run netted like a brain,
we have forgotten
about light,
the candles of the sun,
lost emblems of that other world.

Here our only occupation
is patience,
our sometime hope
the whispered news
that one day soon
all this will change
and we will be transmuted,
transposed to pure color—
scarlet, sapphire, gold—
flashing banners in the breeze,
hands stretched upward
signaling to those who pass,
see us,
what we have become,
this bright sensuousness,
unfurling edifice of joy.

KUNDALINI RETURNING AT THE SEASIDE

Ah, well, old rover,
you've come back
again.
Won't ask where you've been,
what company you've been keeping—
whether idling with some other tramp
ready and willing
then wondering what she has
let herself in for,
or else a pious type
praying all night for a sign
which finally comes,
moves in forever demanding ardor,
what then?

Whatever, I'm not jealous,
just glad you're home,
we wantons like
to take what comes,
and seize the day
whether it arrives
dressed in the latest look
or tattered rags,
summoned by some bar room tune
or majestic concert in a hall.
As long as it is the familiar you.
As long as you knock and enter,
take up residence once again

as if you'd never left,
all promises and supplication
as before.

Do not say
this part is
animal,
that spiritual,
this one is higher,
that lower.
Quit trying to find new ways
to cut yourself in two.

When God made you
he blessed every part—
head, soles, and
everything in between.

Then he kissed you again all over
as you were being born.

Now something lives within,
shy serpent self
who stirs and awakens only
from his constant need
to pierce,
to claim,
and let his hidden sweetness
overflow

POEM FOR MARY OLIVER
In gratitude

Because she was willing to do that,
because she was willing to step forth
and be the authentic being,
the true poet,
let the hawk's dark beak,
the bear's ravenous paw,
enter, become part of
who she was...

She spent days
beside the pond,
teeming with its watery life
of dragonflies,
bits of darting light
stitching the surface
into a crisscross
of transparent fire,
the floating blooms
and the oddly engaging
amphibians
with their swollen bellies
and gaping
mouths, their raspy hellos—
who else could cherish these
in such measure?

Reckless nights in the woods
with its stealthy night prowlers
and haunting melodies,
owl screech
and lonely night bird
chorus of snarls and growls
moving near
crackling underbrush
heavy falling limbs
Oh, such sweet terror,
who knows what could have happened
therein
the center
of so much mystery...

All of this
she sang in our ears,
gave to our awakening eyes,
as she became God's messenger,
the vessel to make us see.

AN ANGEL STRAYED INTO TIME
(for Lisel Mueller)

Of the midwinter blooming,
she said it was
"out of phase, like an angel
strayed into time, our world."
And after listening to the concert
(Shubert by Brendel),
she felt she had for two hours
been in "the nowhere
where the enchanted live."

She herself prefers not to overstep,
not to be torn
by the storms of passion,
the earthquakes of revelation.

And so she flirts with it,
the delicate border
where the contraries meet,
this familiar sensed world
and that other, reputed realm
of the unqualified sublime
which beckons, like Avalon,
always just out of reach
in the mists of the never fully discerned.

By nature, a bit shy,

her language is her honed instrument
of exploration,
exposing the hidden unexpecteds
lurking in the midst of the usual.
Words measured, nuanced,
exact,

like a sudden small rainbow of light
which chooses to dance,
momentarily, over a flower
just about to open.

MARK DOTY

(Once during an acupuncture treatment, Mark Doty, a brilliant writer of our time, experienced a full blown mystical vision of the universe as an infinite field of light. He chose not to pursue this esoteric revelation, but to continue in his role as artist and poet of the more tangible realities.)

This man has learned
to hedge his bets,
not to go too far,
stumble into those
fog ridden realms
where the mystics
and crackpots dwell.

His laser eyes
scan a provable landscape,
exposing unexpected vistas,
hidden shadows.

His language is eloquent,
but he risks
only what is verifiable—
the scents and smells
of a summer day,
the revealed connections
of events and their origins,
pleasurable insights
into the hidden world
of a threaded reality

which startles but never stuns,
all well within the comfort zone
of our accepted possible.

His exquisite script
claims the world
as form,
thing seen anew
from a different angle,
something we covet,
yearn to hold close again.

ROTHKO

Something about the way
the paint moves
across the surface,

how the light strikes
the layers, the unfolding
path of the formless form.

how he poured
his soul (unproved)
into his work
like glaze

abandonment of the extraneous,
compression to source.

The invisible
struggling
to be seen,
before the waters and the land
were parted.

What energy possessed
this swimmer in the wine-dark sea?
How did the brain ignite
and so surrender,
unveil
this forgotten knowing?

POEMS FOR MIRABAI

1. THE BESOTTED FOLLOWER

To dance in this field
of radiance,
what will I give?

My good name, long since
taken from me.
My tattered robe,
with mud for its hem—
oh, no, haven't seen it for days.
Family, friends—all have vanished,
have turned their faces away.

Still, I dance,
moving this way or that,
following the inner currents,
celebrating the hidden bliss,
my lone partner
Krishna and his silver flute,
that music which plays only for those
willing to be shattered
again and again,
ravished by sweetness,
torn by that joy.

2. ONLY THIS

Out of it, you say,
See her, she is mad,
her sighs and curious movements,
her smile and absent gaze,
she is a lunatic lost
in an imagination gone astray.

This world and its occupations,
its priorities and needs,
these alone exist,
only these are real.

In it, you say,
This, yes, this,
always without ceasing,
this is the only thing
I desire,
the single gift
I want.

MY TRIDENT AND BELL

I am willing
to go down.
I am willing to be
the crazed saint,
the raving mystic
babbling of God.

I am ready to invite
Shiva
into my bed.

Soon I shall cover
my body with ashes,
put a mark on my forehead,
go into the streets
with my trident
and bell.

You will not
know me then.
You will wonder
who I am,
what I am saying,
what became of the person
who used to live
at my former address.

NIGHT AFTER NIGHT

Make love your business.
— Rumi

I have made love
my business
and where has it
gotten me?

Nothing I would
care to share
with others.

Only this being
alone
night after night
with the Beloved,
faint with kisses.
It never ends.

THIS GIFT

This gift you have given me
who can say its value?
I can only clutch it
wait for something more.

***

How is it
that you keep returning,
even after the candle has
long since died away,
even when I have given up
the remains of my longing
and gone to dream
once more alone in my bed?

***

These words you keep slipping
into my mouth,
this throat kiss,
this terrible knowing
of what it is to be loved...
Nevertheless, I will keep returning,
even if I still, after so many years,

do not know your name,
where you are coming from
how to follow you when you leave.

***

Now you are telling me
it doesn't really matter
how long this affair
has gone on,
when it began,
who made the first move.
You say this moment
is pure honey.
Drink.

ARE YOU WILLING!

The ascent to Joy
Is itself the transforming
Of fear into LOVE.
Marina Gamble

Are you willing to ascend to this joy?
It will tear you, rend you,
shatter your limbs
and fling them
into the sky
like dry sticks of straw
caught on the wind.

At times you will think you are drowning,
tossed in the furious ocean of longing,
at others
that you are scorched
by unseen fires,
flare of passion.

Do you imagine you will
then remember who you are?
Why you began this journey?
Think well
before you enter this path.

Consider the price
of a single kiss.

SUFIS

Only yesterday I swore
to give up all this daylight
love play,
to get down to business,
early rising,
travel over rough trails,
brown bread and hard cheese
for lunch,
only water to drink.

But already this wisp of song,
these turning dancers
with skirts unfolding
like flowers awakened,
or birds spreading their white
or scarlet wings
in their flurry of ascent—
these have glazed my eyes,
carried me into
that other place,
secret trysting spot
familiar love ground...

Sometimes I just stand here
thinking about you
and I disappear.

***

Listen, listen...
can you hear those honey drops fall
from the mouth of God?

Can you feel the rose
opening in your spine?
Whatever you were before,
now you are only this.

***

Do you want
words
or feelings?
Or are they melted together
like the love streaming from your lover's
eye, meeting the love
pouring from your own?

***

Does anyone else
feel this love?
Like the breath
of a thousand rose gardens
dreaming that they are petals
crushed in God's hand.

***

Is this from this world
or another?
do these words have meanings
or are they mere love cries
from that one
come to kiss you awake again.
God has a thousand names
and I but one tongue
to tell them.

***

Some call me a wastrel,
some a wanton.
All I want
is to dance this dance
we do so well together.

***

Are you looking for the goddess?
She is
the lash on God's eye,
the hand stroking your velvet flesh alive,
the pearl
you found under your tongue
this morning.

***

All this time together
and still you have not told me
your name,
who I am,
where this journey leads.

YOUR OCEAN
(for Patricia)

Do you think such things
are not possible?
Have you looked in a mirror
lately,
seen the face you have become,
this sun-marked visage,
this God shine parable
named you?

***

When you are in love
you do not say
you are near love
or beside love,
or seeking to know
love's truth.

You say you are in love.

Never mind how you got here.
This is your ocean.
Drown in it.

***

Now we are birthing

not just ourselves,
but the world and all its beings.

We are women squatting together
in a delivery circle,
bringing forth this new age,
this squalling,
wriggling time
ready to leap out,
shout its name aloud.

***

This canopy of words—
this outpour of sayings—
they help us to unlock
the glaciers of the mind,
unfurl the tight knit banners
waiting to proclaim presence,
capture us, make love.

***

Think about who you are.
Think of all that was rolled into your skin
even before you were born.

What will you do with these gifts
these sacraments waiting for you
to claim them?

TERESA IN ECSTASY

Bernini saw it.
Gave us
the woman in
her full inscrutable passion.

The angel stands near,
piercing her breast with his arrow,
lancing her heart
to love.

Nothing
in chapel or cell,
no soft telling of beads
or whispered hours
prepared her for this moment,
readied her for this time.

How, we wonder,
can she abide
this fiery rapture,
relentless agony of ascent?

How endure
such final fusion,
this sudden annihilation
into light?

THE STAGES OF BLISS

Once yogi returned,
I sat on the floor,
ankles crossed,
did puja with bells and clasped hands—
asanas were the key—
heavy bliss flows stirring
like rivers of love,
everything for the god/goddess
who had come at last.

Then I became music—
kirtans, bhajans,
Brahms,
honey in the throat,
the hands.
Sacred sounds
to stroke the hidden
centers awake,
angels
kissing me alive.
Who could refuse
such favor?

Then it was Buddha
beckoning,
thangka on my wall,
image bringing ineffable joy.

I bowed and rapture
flooded my crown,
my body.
I withstood it to the edge of feeling
as I rose toward some other realm.
Was I still there?

Now I stand
in the center of silence,
soft wind stirring leaves,
moon stilling the waters.
I bow quietly,
move little,
Light flowing
in gentle pulses,
a subtle sweetness,
the other telling me once more
who I am.

WHAT THE GODS REQUIRE:
THE PROPHET
(for Andrew)

They want you as their
Sacrifice.

The lamb that lies down,
full of arrows,
roses blooming scarlet
at every opening.

They want you to speak endlessly,
your mouth, your throat
an instrument for that
which is hidden, has never been
said.

They want you to be available.
Time is short.

They want you to be forgetful
of everything that went before,
even your triumphs and accolades,
your ribbons of celebration.

They want you to continue forever,
like a pure ray of light

extending into the unseen infinite,
which does not bend, nor remember
its beginnings,
nor even when it passed over
into that other realm.

FINALLY WE TOOK AN AXE

For years we circled
our hidden chamber
seeking a way out.

Nothing sufficed:
Not prayers,
nor supplications,
not knees against stone
nor heavy penance
of nails and shirts of hair.

Finally, we took an axe
and broke through to God.
At first we were blinded by the splendor,
the majesty and
shining raiment.
We crept closer
and raised our head a little.

Then a voice said,
where have you been,
my dear one?
I have been waiting for you
for so many years.

I know all about
living in caves
with candles and scented prayers,
crossing the desert which never ends
seeking the One who is always near,
spreading my deerskin
in the forest depths
where the spirits of the blue-bodied gods
hang like shadows of watching birds.

With the others, I wove
a story of connection,
something mysterious and inscrutable
we called to appear
with our fires and recitations
our songs of supplication and praise.
A voice spoke through us
as we chanted our words
and the centuries passed.

This time I came in other guise.
I roamed the avenues,
mingled in the market
with the restless crowds,
watched and listened in alarm
as the world reeled and
spun down

toward its approaching dark.

And I saw that this
was the time
to take on new knowledge,
move through different space,
hear with unfamiliar ears,
speak with strengthened voice,
atoms transfigured,
senses restrung,
it is happening to us all,
blazing illumination,
beauty erupting in the midst of despair,
splendor unveiled
on a field of pain,
we are being filled with light
we do not comprehend
lifted toward essence
assaulted by nameless love
at this juncture
of the finalities,
intersection of the unimaginables.
This is why we came.

LIVING WITH BUDDHA

(Recently I purchased a Buddhist thangka, which seems to possess special powers of awakening the inner vibrations. This poem is about this experience.)

1.

I never expected this.
As always, it was just the music and me,
the vibrations coming on like waves
ruffling the shore.
And then the Unseen came,
taking my breath—
sly cat circling the cradle
where the naked baby lies—
and suddenly
you appeared,
radiant being
lit from within
like an icon set in a temple
incandescence lighting
your face, your breast.
Now there was the outer image,
and this inner brightness as well—
what was I to do?

2.

True, there had been a time of preparation, a leading up—
for days, Tibetan music
with its raucous gongs and drums
beating the blood

to a kind of inner frenzy,
slow movement whipping the vibrations
to a pitch,
like a lash
over the waves,
everything pulsating,
bliss, they call it,
who can give it a name?

3.

And then the day when many Buddhas
came within
in geometric procession,
appearing one behind the other
like figures in a text
on perspective,
showing how objects maintain power
even as they diminish
I couldn't even move.

4.

I found it there days earlier,
on the wall of the import store,
holding me in its gaze,
Buddha in a wall painting,
a kind of scroll
with the Teacher
captured in the design,
they name it a thangka,
majestic presence

calling me.

But I didn't yield.
I left empty handed.

5.
But later
I returned,
telling myself,
If it's still there,
I'll take it,
if not, I'll simply say
it wasn't meant to be
and muse on nonattachment.

It was waiting.
I ran my hand over the face
and felt sweetness
ripple like musk-scented breezes
over my wrist.
I'll take it, I said.

6.
Next morning,
when I bowed
to this image
on my wall,
the energies
pulsed so sweet and strong
I almost could not stand.

First, my head
was blessed
as if his aura
touched my own,
then body, legs,
arms, and hands
all began quietly to move,
to slowly dance,
and I became a turning
Buddha field
of light,
my limbs like blossomings of
love,
some kind of nectar.
I could not even ask
what was happening.
I could only
become
whatever it was.

7.

And so each morning,
there was boundless bliss
and inner teachers came,
each day someone new.
I gave them nicknames
to keep them straight:
"Sturdy Boy" or "Master Chi"
or "Ting Mao" with his flowing
sleeves and fan,

Tara with my mother's face—
so many, all to lead me
in my morning rite,
new movements, new postures
I was easily led, bliss currents streaming.

8.

When I moved in close
to get a better look,
the Buddha field
surrounded me.
I turned my face gently
right and left,
I felt its soft stroke
along my cheeks.
I bowed
and began my movements
once again.

How many minutes
could I stay
in this electric clasp?
How long survive
in this dense
torrent of love?

9.

High, high.
Were these the vibrations
of the outer realms,

the place of gods and
deities of every kind,
the supramundane,
suprahuman,
other worldly
spirits from the
secret spheres?

When Zeus came down to Semele,
she vanished in a flash.

Who can withstand
such all-devouring love,
who is willing
to be pierced again and again by light,
light purified at source?

First, you arrived
like a flower
lit from within,
holding its own sun.

I let your
multiple form
inhabit my mind.

Now you are an image
poised
against my wall.

Each morning
I stand before you, bow,
move about a bit,
while you watch quietly
in your steady pose,
you the unchanging,
compassionate wisdom,
easy love.

I WILL

If you want me
to fling myself in,
yes, I will do that
this fire does not burn.

If you want me to linger
along the edges
in a stance of contemplation,
probing the Mystery—
oh, what does it mean?

If you want me to
speak to multitudes,
to utter
your hidden syllables
to masses of hearers,
I will clear my throat
and begin.

If you want me to be still,
say nothing,
eyes shut to all
but where the radiant
darkness dwells,
I will open my heart
to silence,
let my spirit
swell with compassion,
become love.

PART 3

The Ley Lines of The Soul

POEMS OF ECSTASY AND ASCENSION
2012

LEY LINES
(Definition)

Ley lines are invisible energy lines that run below
the surface of the Earth and mark various sacred sites
and settlements along their trajectory.

I think of them as the unseen threads that connect
each of us to others as well as to divine source.

WHAT IS SACRED POETRY?

Sacred poetry is the ongoing effort of the soul to capture
in syllables the relation of the self to the larger reality
which we call the divine. It seeks to outline in graspable
ways the connection of the mortal to the immortal,
the confined to the boundless. It is the arriving spirits'
lament for the lost paradise, and its celebration of
recurrent joy at its earthly home.

Poetry issues from the realm of the mysterious,
that region which resides within us all but which we
can explore only through indirect and imprecise means.
This realm is not available for direct scrutiny.
Occasionally we catch strains of its distant song,
or stumble upon fragments of its secret messages.
When this happens, we call it a poem.

Poetry weaves the ley lines of the soul.

BEFORE

Before I was named I belonged to you.
— Rilke

Wherever I was, hidden in your thigh,
a sycamore seed waiting
in earth,
a thought preparing to leap forth,
I had no name.
My body had no shape.
My eyes were not yet
opened.
Even my face was dark.
What are the features
of that which does not exist?
Nonetheless, I was yours,
an unmarked impulse,
a treasure you carried
like a charm
hung from your vest,
before you sent me
down.

WHO YOU ARE

How the body is put together,
with its tender fastenings,
its mysterious openings,
its muscles working in
smooth coordination
to convey it,
where it wishes to go,
how it changes
from year to year,
from day to day,
its cells working in collusion
to carry it always
into a new configuration,
how the face communicates
its signals
wherever it goes,
whether it is
happy or sad
or puzzled
or plotting,
how the inner and outer,
organs and coverings are part
of the same being,
the same oneness
that is bound together
to make the unique creation,
the one combination

that is you,
present here, now,
spirit's abode, soul's habitation,
never to be encountered
again in time's endless cycles.

HOW TO SEE AN ANGEL

Stand very still.
Don't breathe,
or if you do,
do it silently.

Be in a familiar place,
or else a new place
which feels familiar:

Under a tree by
running water.
Or else in a church
Or temple,
where vibrations of
the holy still linger
in the air.

Incense and candles are
fine,
but not required.

If you know a prayer
or a mantra,
this is the time.

Music will help.
Especially kirtans

or hymns.

Look around
for bits of color,
small flashes of light.

Close your eyes
for one brief moment,
then open and turn very slowly.

Listen for something that
sounds like a wooden flute
playing in the distance.

You will feel a
quiet breeze pass over you.
Your cells will brighten,
and you will give a little sigh.

That is when it will happen.
There will be a soft rush of wings
a blur of shining movement.
Everything will light up
as if you are standing
in a cloud of sweet feeling.

Now look straight ahead—
an image will appear
at the corner of your eye,
white wings hovering against

a field of blue and gold.

Your heart will open
and you will become
as if two lovers kissing.

When you awaken,
you will find
a single feather
in your hand.

WHATEVER YOU OFFER

Whatever you offer me,
I will take it.

I don't need bribes
to swallow
the bread and honey of your love.

This wine needs no water
to wash it down.

Even if we must perform
the many labors,
or huddle in
the darkened corners
of the caves
for eons
as the silence thickens
and the glaciers
gather.

This is what we have
hungered for
for so many days,
for so many lifetimes.

THE SEEKER ATTEMPTS TO RETURN

I could, of course, put
a mark
on my forehead
(and don't think
I wouldn't like
to do this)

or I might wander
about in a robe
of saffron or maroon
(and never believe
I wouldn't wish
to clothe myself this way).

I could stand beneath
a tree
and recite ancient verses,
give blessings as
someone with strange eyes
fondles a flute
or a stringed instrument
nearby
(and I would do this gratefully,
indeed I would).

I could infuse the crowd
with sweetness,

love energy from God
and watch them cry out,
and fall to the ground.
Now I have only silence
sometimes these words,
dream passages
from that other world
that I say to myself
at night.
Shanti, shanti, shanti

WHATEVER YOU DO

Whatever you do,
don't waste your time
struggling with issues
about "faith" and
whether "the Other" is real
or not.

Do not worry about
your own existence—
whether you are palpable
or just a mirage
floating in a mirror.

When the worthies
begin debating such things inside
the temple,
do not bow and listen.
Run outside,
rattle the windows,
storm the doors,
let the music of light
come in.

Better still,
turn them out
into the sun,
point their solemn faces

toward the trees
blooming in fall's
swelling luminosity,
let them see how
brilliant

a leaf
falling gracefully
into its new incarnation,
how majestic the limbs
in their bright emerging configurations.

THE MYSTERY

Some come at it
with weights and measures,
some waving a sieve.

Some sing to it,
ballads and carols,
hoping to coax forth
its hidden center,
unwind the sheath
of who it is.

Some tap on it,
or deal heavy blows
with hammers,
trying to smash
its thick shield,
force it to bow down.

Some seek ways to clamber in,
explore its hidden vaults
and chambers.

Some lie down beside it,
breathe its cool scent,
become its own self.

BETROTHED

So at the end of the day, we give thanks for being betrothed to the unknown.
—John O'Donohue

However one looks at it,
it was not easy—
that bridal night,
mingling of self
and the unknown who appeared.

Everything took place
in secrecy and silence,
at the hidden center,
the core where presence
begins.

How do you mate
with something unseen
become one
with what has no form or name?

The days were filled with sweetness
and tumult,
nights so intense
that passion itself
became too pale a word.

The world unfolded
in endless celebration,

a constant feast to which
the heart said yes,
the spirit yearned.

Now, old lovers,
we live quietly,
sometimes meet
and nod in recognition,
remembrance of that special time
when we no longer knew
who was lover, who beloved.

BETROTHED
(for the Beloved Within)

What I can tell you
is only about
the bliss.

The gurus and the priests,
they have their notions
and their theories.

It may all of it be true,
every single particle and proclamation.

But I know nothing
about such notions as these.
I know only the blinding moment when the Lover arrives,
the sadness of
goodbye.

No one told me
how
to do this,
or how to share it
abroad with others.
Mine is a solitary
joy,
a single path
to the gateless
gate.

Nobody understands this
unless they have been there,
traveled this rock-strewn road,
fallen into this deep well.

How could you know how it is
to have your heart
eaten by a lion
unless you had heard
the lion's roar,
felt his clasp
upon your throat?

What could you imagine
about lost angels
floating down
on pulsing streams of light
unless your bed
was covered
in feathers
when you awoke?

THE SURPRISE

She says, I am not ready for this.
It says, you have always been
ready for this.

She says, I don't know where
this is coming from.
It says, you know exactly where
this is coming from.

She says, I don't know how
to do this.
It says, you have always known
how to do this.

She says, what will happen
when you leave?
It says, I will never leave.
I am your body, brain,
and blood,
I am the One of all.
I am your true core.

OUT OF NOWHERE

When you first came
I was not prepared,
lightning flash of love
arriving out of nowhere.

Now you enter more stealthily.
Sometimes you have stayed
the night
and I did not even know.

I still am not used
to your presence,
lodger who
leaves no sign,
pays no rent.

FOR SO MANY YEARS

How could I have known
this marriage would endure so long.
That you would remain faithful
for so many years.

I think this union
was meant to last.
Year after year:

your secret kisses,
my amazed silence.

LIKE A MONGOLIAN

Now you are arriving
just anywhere.

Like a Mongolian herdsman
who tackles his bride
on the steppe
and plants his flag to say,
"Here we are!"

Your horse, my mare,
what a combination.

THIS LOVE

can consume you,
devour you,
drag you to the depths
where pearls float in the eyes
of the lost fishers,
blast you into
the outer regions
where there is no sound
but the frantic beating
of your own heart,
break you like brittle clay,

bend you like
molten iron,
wrap you around
your own belly,
turn your face
toward what
is ever shining,
waiting
for you to see.

*(The fourth line echoes the well-known Shakespearean image included by
Eliot in "The Waste Land": "Those are pearls/ that were his eyes.")*

THE BECKONING

You called me
and I came down,
small soul wrapped
in the folds of the dark flower.

I arrived not knowing
where I had been,
whose voice had summoned,
why I had come.

How could I foresee
that this unfolding
would arrive
in such bliss,
body awakening again
to its own beginnings?

How could I guess
it would carry such pain,
always the throb of grief
pulsing through
the vein of joy?

WHAT ?

For a long while,
bliss
lay hidden
inside me,
bright flame within a dark rock.

Now it is pain,
light playing over water.

Are these two sides
of the same coin,
different ends of the same rainbow?

Two mysteries
wrapped around
each other
in a single packet,
waiting to be
opened.

STILL MORE LOVE POEMS FOR THE INVISIBLE

1. WHAT I HAVE GIVEN YOU

What I have given you
is everything.
What you have given me
is everything
in return.

Now we are one being,
both of us giving
and receiving,
bound together—
flame and candle—
as before.

2. ONLY THE LOVEMAKING

The Lover is always beside you,
waiting.

The Lover is patient,
like a devoted friend,
or someone who gave you food
long ago.

But you must give the signal.
You must say,
"Now, I am ready.

Come to my chamber at midnight."

The Lover will come,
still invisible,
still without a name.
Only the lovemaking
will be real.

3. WHATEVER YOU DO

Whatever you do,
don't tell anyone
about this.
They make laws against
such alliances,
put people in prison cells,
lock them away
like shadows.

They do not wish
to hear our story,
our tale must not be told.
Except, of course,
to those ready to listen,
the ones also enfolded
in this precious cloak,
tapestry embroidered
of God's flesh.

PARTICLES DANCING

We are all writing God's poem.
—Anne Sexton

We are all
writing God's poem,
inscribing it onto our bodies,
breathing it into our cells.

Night and day
we make love with the light.
Where it is taking us,
we dare not ask.

We know only
that this is the love
that makes us
remember our beginnings,
particles dancing
in the holy fire.

HYMN TO THE NAMELESS ONE

It is true, yes,
that still I cannot name you.
Nor can I describe
your face,
never having seen it.
What I know is
that you have come
again and again,
often as something called
bliss,
or as landscapes pregnant with joy,
as sound like music
drifting from a shell.

Now as the year swings down,
and the darkness encloses
even the smallest bird,
the largest animal,
and we, too, enter the hour
when everything is falling once more
into the twilight
of not knowing,
what we ask is that
you be with us,
not as a pillar of fire
nor a blaze across
the heavens,

but like water
at rest in a pitcher
which catches the morning light
and is filled
with its own radiance.

Everything swept away.

What fire did not
devour,
flood consumed.

Nothing left but this
purified field,
this immaculate transparency.

The place where I
wait
for God.

It is never too late.
Even if you have trudged
through snow and ice
for a thousand miles
and still have not arrived.
Even if the map is lost
and the compass broken.
When the eagle who is
supposed to guide you
goes off on a tangent
of its own
and you know you are,
once again, deserted,
do not fall into
the pit of despair.
It will return,
brighter than ever.
There will be feather tokens
falling down.

Nothing is irredeemable.
Nothing is lost forever.
Be guided by the stars.
Let the moonlight
direct your steps.

There will be a path

which will open
in the forest.
The treasure which is yours
is waiting.

IN A STRANGE TONGUE

Say you went on a journey
to a place
that was not on the map,
saw many strange sights there—
temples made of jade,
elephants with tusks of gold—
made love every night
with a different stranger.

Say you woke up one day,
found gold dust
in your pocket,
a bracelet of jade
wrapped around you wrist,
all else gone.

Who would listen
to your story?
Who would believe
your traveler's fairy tale?
Now you are
the outcast other,
the changeling
come home,
the revenant tapping
at the window,
speaking in a strange tongue
which no one understands.

AFTER

There is one thing certain.
Once you have stood
in the midst of that
searing flame,
been struck down
to earth
like a pilgrim
entered by light at last
and have lain there,
waiting,
not quite certain—

how can you ever know again
what it is
not to be blinded by the light,
never to have gone there
to the top of the snow-hung peak
and felt that nameless something
descend onto your shoulders,
your breast,
even as you bent forward
in disbelief.

Sometimes I think
it might have been easier,
not to have been touched
by that stroke of fire,
not to have been ignited,
like Moses' bush, by that
flame that does not burn,
nor to have been lifted
to those storied heavens
where the gods look down
and never speak.

What does it mean to die
before death comes?
To arrive when the journey
has barely just begun?

How would life have been,
infused with the ordinary,
days worn thin with repetition,
children crying in the night,
bread rising, the wine jug filled,
as if by doing again and again
one might progress toward
an unknown goal?

On the chapel wall,

God stretches out his hand to Adam,
and Adam comes alive,
ready to be born once more.

How did you greet
that angel who arrived?
How did you bear it,
that shock of light,
when God entered every cell?

EVERYTHING MOVING

Who am I to say
how this world
is put together,
how the seams and ridges
fit,
why the waters heave
and flow.

Only the architect
knows the full extent,
the weights and measures
of
the secret connections
in her palm.

Me, I have my corner
where I dance
to make the hours move,
rhythm to keep the sky alive,
hold Earth and moon in place,
everything turning,
expanding sphere of light.

AS SILK TO COARSE FIBER
(For the Beloved Within)

After a time,
the awakening process settles down.
It is no longer strong feelings you want,
but something much
more subtle, more delicate,
refined.

As silk to coarse fiber,
as aged wine to heavy ale—

Something like
gentle breezes
after a strong wind.

The branches no longer
thrash and toss wildly,
threatening to break entirely
or demolish the houses
huddled below.

Even the clouds are still,
everything waiting
for this next new birth.

This is merely a metaphor—

how it felt in the beginning,
how it is between us now.

(This poem is intended to describe the Kundalini process, which often begins in a rather stormy process, with much surging energy and many "ups and downs." As the years pass, things do indeed settle down, with the bliss flows becoming ever softer, arriving in subtle pulsations such as you would not have been able to experience at the outset.)

If you want to feel
the sweet light
flow over your body,
then give yourself to light.

If you want
to taste the secret honey,
you must allow your throat
to open.

Moth to candle,
straw to flame,
you are nothing but
materials for burning.

are enigmatic, ethereal, ineffable—
as hard to capture
as catching the leaping fountain of God
in a teacup,
the flight of the eagle
into the sun,
the thunder of hooves
on the prairie
when the ears are closed
with candle wax.

The Soul arrives
in its own good time,
lets you know it is there
with a kiss on the lips,
a hand against your
breast.

If you can feel this,
then you know
that the Soul has come at last,
bringing its own
true gifts,
its inexplicable mercy.

THE AWAKENING

You never knew
where it came from.
Later some said
past life,
some voted for purity
in this
(though you knew better).

In any event,
it was your time.
All the conditions were ripe, floating like feathers
on a stream
to a preselected destination.

No one was there
to lead you.
Not even a person to tell,
friend or loved one,
attentive listener.
So you kept everything
locked in,
secret treasure
hidden in the
dark recesses
of your personal closet,
like a forbidden novel,

a store of some
illegal substance or thing.

Meanwhile,
you kept your appointments
each morning
with the unknown suitor,
the one you called the Beloved,
who had no name,
formless other.

As the years passed,
you came to know
one another well in a fierce union,
flame of terror and bliss,
and the silence deepened.

You never discovered
why it happened,
what it meant.

Even now
it continues
in its own inscrutable
way.

Moment to moment
of the indecipherable.

DANCING WITH THE GREAT LION

I keep circling you,
pacing, checking
my watch.

You keep eyeing me,
growling in your throat,
saying, *Hurry, it's time.*

How long have we been
doing this dance?
How many lifetimes
have we moved like this
together?

You suggesting,
me nodding,
both of us
waiting
to see what will happen.

GOING BEYOND

Once you arrive at the crossroads,
you must choose
from three paths.

One is the path of fire.
To enter it,
you must take off
all your clothes,
fasten your tongue
to the roof of your mouth,
shut your eyes,
no longer breathe.

The second is the way of water.
To go here,
you must relinquish your boundaries,
make of yourself a drop of rain,
a splash of ocean water,
a handful drawn from a well.

The last is the journey by night
along Earth's ridges and descents.
This will take a long time.
It will be filled with terrors:
fuming dragons,
monsters threatening.
When you finally arrive,

you will be nothing
but air,
mist,
burning sunlight—
you will be other.

PART 4

Penelope's Loom

POEMS OF TURNING MATTER INTO SPIRIT

2012

PENELOPE'S LOOM

My specialty
is waiting.
I sat here at my loom
winding and unwinding
my cloth
by day and by night
for endless years
while the grapes ripened
and fell.

Meanwhile the suitors
pressed me:
Some wanted
my possessions,
some my love,
all demanded that I constantly
attend.

Sometimes I got distracted,
engaged in a bit
of dalliance,
went too far
once or twice
but regretted it
later.

How could I remember

what had shaped my life
so long ago,
even before I arrived?
It was all now like a shadow
coming into focus now and again,
then disappearing into the
moonlight once more.

The name of what I waited for
was the voyager,
the other part of my spirit/self
gone astray for so long.
The voyager traveled many lands,
had many adventures
to distract,
finally returned
and claimed me,
and I at last was united with
what I had longed for
for so long,
forgotten fragment,
journey's end.

(In Homer's great epic called The Odyssey, Penelope is the faithful wife
of Odysseus, who is gone for 20 years fighting (and then returning from)
the Trojan War. To fend off the many suitors who want to marry her in his
absence, she weaves a cloth each day, and unravels it at night, promising to
make her choice once her weaving is finished. This poem is a retelling of the
story—how we each long to be reunited with that part of ourselves that is
missing or forgotten.)

THIS BEAD OF LIGHT

There could, I suppose,
have been nothing.
Only void and darkness,
and possibly
not even that.
Just extension
into an infinity
of space
that enclosed
emptiness.

Instead
there was this explosion. This bead of light
that suddenly
flew forth
in all directions,
dispersing,
congealing,
becoming
a billion universes,
of which
ours is one:
the place
we found each other,
met and said goodbye,
made and broke
our promises,
wept
and came together again.

THE GOD PARTICLE

They call it the God particle.
No one had ever seen it,
but they say it is what
holds everything together,
the glue of the universe.

This all pervasive
binder of creation
can't be located,
though they keep searching
with their colliders
and fine instruments,
night after night,
through the long hours,
the many years.

Some claim they have detected
traces,
but the claim is
still not fully certain,
anecdotal evidence unconfirmed
by independent observation.

Maybe they are searching
in the wrong places, all this
insistent scanning of the
infinitely small

to explain
the infinitely huge.
How did this world
of things
emerge from the dark bead of nothing?
Have they not heard
of the original trembling,
the first heaving
of primal rapture?

(Note: Early texts of Kashmiri Shaivism explain that the world of matter derives from supreme consciousness, which first vibrates at an infinitely high rate, then slows into progressively slower and thicker vibrations, out of which tangible, perceptible forms emerge. This "primordial and unimpeded light of consciousness...is totally free and pellucid, ever expanding into waves of completely new bliss." See The Yoga of Vibration and Divine Pulsation by Jaideva Singh, foreword by Paul E. Muller-Ortega.)

EVER ARRIVING

At the still point of the turning world
there the dance is...
Except for the point, the still point,
there would be no dance,
and there is only the dance.
—T. S. Eliot

I think of it
as the Swirling Radiance,
movement that never ceases,
ever arriving
from the last moment
of eternity,
the plundered second
of all that will ever be.

And you, here,
are at the midpoint,
the demarcation
of what has always been
and what is perpetually approaching,
your seeing is that which sustains,
carries forth,
enables.

You are the perpetual witness,
heaven's link to time.
If you listen, you can
almost hear it swish
as it goes by.

THEORIES

And now there are, it seems,
theories of everything—
of love, of death, of sleep,
of winning or losing,
of the origin of stars,
or where we might have come from
so many years ago.

Dostoevsky abhorred those systems
in which the so-called rational
governs human affairs,
philosophies which ignore spirit
and human feeling,
those inner lights
which deliver us
from false assumptions,
and thus save us from betraying
others and ourselves.

Now science posits entire
universes beside and within
our own,
parallels where time, space,
the arc of enlightenment,
the dark night of the soul's eclipse
are all happening constantly, contiguously,
perhaps even in our own living space,

all undetected by our shrunken senses.
But if we cannot see it,
how can we believe?

Something shadows us,
insists on asking
what about all that nightly going
hither and thither,
ghost forms streaming out of the body,
toward the light
and back again,
skating between time present
and the lost ages
of tribal memory.
And of course, accounts
of angels, strange encounters
with curious forms, from dwarfs
to demons,
stories of those who travel timelessly
from one spot to another,
see great distances,
or appear in many places
all at the same moment.

That most celebrated man
of recent years,
with his famous halo of glinting hair
gave us
theories of the stars,
the planets hung in their twirling spaces,

their dizzying rounds,
but nothing on this,
our constant dilemma,
who, in fact,
we truly are,
into what other universe our journey
takes us now.

WHO WE ARE

Some are air,
flitting and sailing
from place to place,
never settled,
felt only after they have passed by.

Others are like water,
constantly flowing,
taking on new forms,
parting sometimes
to embrace small islands
in their path,
or else taking the shape of
containers which define them:
vase, bank, or shore.

Earth holds fast,
never stirs
unless it is touched
by things outside:
hurricanes, machines, floods,
falling trees.
Its devotion
keeps the world steady.

Fire devours all,
orange tongues flaring,

brilliance of creator/destroyer,
begetting beauty,
turning everything back
to origins,
earth, air, water of the beginning.

THE CAVE PAINTERS OF LASCAUX

Certainly,
they were more alive.
Their eyes beheld
what has long since
vanished
from the scan of
our narrow
view,
their flesh quivered
with delight
or pain
in ways we can
only imagine.

When they went
out for the hunt,
magic carried them
through,
their wives and old ones
mumbling incantations over
the fire
as they stalked
their sacred prey
with weapons
carved from flint,
from wood.

When they entered
the caves,
they carried
their primal powers
with them,
wreathing the walls
with delicate beasts
who were their friends
as well as their sustenance.

Red, ocher, gold—
they knew how to mix
and apply their vivid
tones like any skillful artist, capturing
the color of flame,
color of earth.

But it was the vitality
of the image itself
that mattered,
the animal
now rendered in its
essential form,
unchanging, immortal,
energies streaming
from the artist's moving hands
onto the cave walls,
into the darkest recesses,
creature and human
again becoming one.

THE PHOTOGRAPHER
(for Patricia)

She has transcended body,
left it behind.
She lives in a brain-ferment,
a buzzing hive of mind,
a tossing sea of perception.

She gathers fragments
of the presented world
and translates them
into a new medium,
a cosmos of images
held in a different frame.

In this uncovered order,
sun and darkness meet,
old and unaccustomed bleed into
one another's space.

She is the eternal creator,
eyeing, composing, unmaking,
turning life over
into new soil, new beginnings,
unexpected revelation.

Ah, Beethoven,
with your madness
and your grief,
your raging tones
and blocked ears
that shut out
all but your fury and
your sorrow,
your
untamed notes
that defied it all,
even the gods,
the forces
that would drag you down,
nothing to love
but the fickle boy,
not even clean linen
or food,
just the pulsing
heartbeat of the universe
throbbing constantly
in your seething brain.

"MY JOB IS TURNING MATTER INTO SPIRIT"

Consider Louise Nevelson
who spoke these words,
how she kept on going,
how the shapes and forms
inhabited her dreams at night,
her hours of waking,
how they kept tumbling forth—
spheres, rectangles, squares,
complex shapes
of pentagons, tetrahedrons,
things for which we
have no names—
all emerging
like images
from a photographic
solution
rising to the surface,
arranging themselves
in relationship
until what she had
was something
borrowed from
the beginning
of creation,
original form
coming into being.

All right,
I did it.
In a time
when despair
was the fashion,
when nothing was approved
unless it confirmed
the catastrophe
unfolding all around,
when anyone who was the least
cosmopolitan (and all poets imagine
they are the most cosmopolitan
of the species) sang
from the safe distance
of ironic detachment,
I played innocent,
affirmed the unattainable,
looked heavenward
(that old cliché)
for inspiration.

When others retreated
into the safety of the
personal,
the quotidian world
of the everyday familiar
(my youth,

my father,
my wife,
my child)
I abandoned
such themes
for a broader canvas.

Even God was allowed
to enter and play a role.
Even the ultimate
crept
into
my verses.
I had seen
what I had seen,
felt what I had felt.
Now I knew what I knew, a
nd would not deny
it,
even though it
dimmed my light
in all but the smallest
circles,
even though my name
was only
a whisper.

SEA CHANGE

I do not know
how I got caught up
on this wave,
bounding and tossing,
always farther out to sea,
always being shaped
into a new image,
meanwhile
my other self
watching not so much
in fear
but in curiosity and a casual interest
from the shore,
thinking,
Yes, now I am becoming
who I truly am,
go ahead,
pound and mold me,
make me whatever it is
I am supposed to be
now at this time, in this place,
neither of which is locatable
on time pieces or maps,
both together forming a matrix
constantly shifting,
as if it can't quite make up its mind
how it wants to go,
or else has a purpose
that no one else
can see.

Everyone wants to talk
about Persephone.
Especially the poets.
How she was grabbed
and carried off,
how she was kept in darkness
so many months,
while her mother searched everywhere,
waited for her darling
to come home.

Some say
the daughter
liked what had happened
(you know the story,
how women really want it
even when they say no),
others claim it is in fact
the mother who is at fault,
that it is she
who drove her daughter
away, forced her to
leave home and
flee into that hidden world,
because of her own impossible
demands.

And then of course
there are those
who read it as a simple
nature myth–three months of fertility and sun,
nine of winter and death
over the land.

What do I think?
I think she is the soul
of each of us,
going down to darkness and obscurity,
overwhelmed by despair,
then resurrecting like a flower
over and over
as the seasons return.

THE UNDER WATER POEMS

1. THE FROND

My job is to yield.
I like to sway,
letting the currents lift me
this way and that.

Even when the mood
is blustery,
when gales sweep
above,
I feel pleasure
in my fringed body,
my elements stroked
as if by an earthly
lover.

2. WHAT THE FISH SAID

I dart hither and thither
as I please.
No one tells me
when to move,
when to pause,
when to hurry
or slow.

I like this sense
of mastery,
of guiding my
own compass,
of being alone
in my search.

What I discover
is mine alone,
to feed hunger
or pass by.

I am the sum
of movement
and grace.
What I value
is freedom,
my right
to choose.

3. WHAT THE EMPTY SHELL SAID

I once held a treasure
in my swirling arms,
a prize to adorn
my secret heart.

Now I am empty,
vacant as a skeleton's eye,
useless as a necklace

that has lost its jewel.

Who will want me now?
Who will admire me,
remember my lost charms?

BELGIAN LACE

Trees like to stay in one place,
go down deep,
drink the milk
of the mother.

Flowers are show-offs,
uncovering their delicate parts
in air,
waiting for the sun
to give them a kiss,
a benediction.

Waves shatter against the rocks,
then make themselves again
as Belgian lace,
fringes of beginnings.

Clouds can't make up their minds,
shift constantly into new patterns,
now a camel,
now a magi or a king.

People in cities
are constantly bumping into one another,
exchanging energy
in secret transactions.

On the cliffs there is silence,
space hurtling down,
distance stretching up,
somewhere the wind calling,
ghosts of fog
drifting in,
bearing the secret
from some other shore.

Then
it appeared,
white magnificence
at the edge
of the shallow pool,
going about its
solitary task,
dipping and lifting
its beak
like a mechanical
toy in a water-filled basin,
seeking sustenance
from the muddy floor,
yet utterly dignified,
absorbed, oblivious
to all of us gathered there
to watch in silence,
the way I suppose
a god might be,
in his composed majesty,
allowing us
to observe her
stark beauty
close at hand,
as if we did not matter,
as if she did not deign
to notice our quiet awe,

until she left,
stretching her great wings
like an archangel taking flight,
then rose until
we could no longer tell
which was bird,
which was sky.

THE CLIMBER

The mountain was steep.
Many had perished
attempting the climb.
But you went ahead anyway,
carrying your backpack
of provisions and tools.
This was the one
you had prepared for
for so many years.
You had planned every move.

At first it didn't seem
so difficult.
You went swinging yourself along,
admiring the view,
all the green valleys and towns
laid out below.

Then things changed.
The slope grew steeper,
the drops more intense.

And finally
you hit the ice—
a thick mantle
of glistening skin,
rocks glazed

like sculptured glass.
Here it was grommets and pickaxe,
a struggle for every inch.
Caution was the word.
The glaciers were fickle,
rousing sometimes
like giant beasts awakening,
advancing in unpredictable ways.

The last stage was where
so many had fallen
into dark chasms,
off the unsteady bridges
or ever slickening surface
only to be discovered years later
dangling in some lost abyss
or not at all.

In some versions of this story
this was where you, too,
plunged to your personal
disaster,
the spot now marked with
stones where later travelers
pause for momentary tribute.

But in this narrative
(the true one)
although you once swung out
you quickly recovered

and clung to the ever
more vertical rock
like a figure painted on a canvas,
a thumbprint on a page,
until you hurled yourself over the rim,
rose and planted your flag,
then waved both arms in triumph
to the unnoticing world below.

WHERE SHADOWS SPEAK

To live like a mole,
you must go underground,
feel your way
along the velvet passages,
only come up to wash your face
in sun.

When raven flies,
he sees everything below—
all the shuddering mountain leaves
falling to the cold ground,
the intricate snow
sculpting the earth
into strange shapes,
dragons and stars.

In the cities,
there is frenzy.
In the pastures,
things dying quietly
or being reborn in green.

Some are caught
between chaos
and stillness,
pulled like loose sails,
don't know which way to turn.

Others hone in,
fix their sights on one thing,
become its texture and form,
the feel of its chiseled surfaces.

Still others are carried to sea
by the riptide in the blood,
out to the deep waters
where the shadows speak to them
of love and fury,
dying for passion,
of never being stranded,
of always going deeper.

(Inspired by a poem by Arthur Sze)

THE BLACK SWAN

Now we know how it was
at Pompeii,
when the volcano
began to rumble
and people looked at each
other in confusion and fear.

Or when the monster wave approached
the shore
of that distant Pacific isle,
and people stopped to gaze in disbelief
and ask one another
what was happening,
no one had ever seen
a wave so big before.
In early Europe, there were
travelers' tales of black swans,
but everyone knew this was a myth,
for swans were never black.
Then one day in Australia,
they found the truth behind the claim,
and people gasped, astonished.

Now a black swan is swimming
into our living rooms,
we are turning our heads,
we stare in disbelief
at this creature formed from impossibility,
this unimaginable darkness.
Which way shall we turn?

TOWARD BETHLEHEM

And what rough beast, its hour come round at last,
slouches towards Bethlehem to be born?
—W. B. Yeats (1865-1939)

Yes, I know.
This is the time
of the second coming.
The great beast lurking,
the savage heart
beating once again.

Somewhere in the desert, for certain,
that blank and pitiless stare.
The haunches moving.
The stealthy advance.

Shall we watch in horror and dismay?
Do we turn away
or witness in silence and despair?

The vision falters,
the image fades again.
That distant struggle
in the clouds of dust--
is this the specter
we ourselves have made,

created from our inner dreamscape
of grasping and desire?
Are we ourselves
the approaching shape
of darkness drawing near?

THE WARRIOR

comes boldly forth
like a closed fist,
saying, I will have it,
it is mine.
I have gone through four zones of fire,
faced five angels,
captured the lost maiden.
Now I wander where I will,
bearing the invisible sign,
carrying the token.
Something from Earth
is rising up,
is swelling through my bones,
coursing calf and thigh,
lifting my arm
into a steady arc,
to drive the arrow home:
I am master of all I do.

THE SKEPTIC

My object is scorn.
Whatever you give me,
I'll pry it open like a box,
releasing the secret within.
Nothing will convince me:

not your evidence, your proofs,
your testimonies or trials.
Everything will by me
be sundered, rent, to expose
the flabby premise,
the flawed foundation:
Behold, you are unmasked!

THE COWARD

I am afraid.
Of everything, even these words,
these audacious strivings
toward what is unformed
and therefore forbidden.

And movement, with its daring gestures.
How can I tear open
a space which
is not mine?

When I meet someone,
I shrink.
They think I am what they are looking at,
the ghost hanging in the shadows,
the eye peering from the cavern wall.
Even an ice axe
could not free my image,
release it from
its brittle pose.

I have given up trying to tell someone.
I have these pictures, these scenes
from the desert where I once lived.
These trinkets,
the vial of dust,
the broken locket
with its wisp of hair;
No one knows my name.

THE CHILD

No one heard my cry.
In silence I moved
from unspoken plea
to unspoken plea,
my eyes frozen,
my mouth taped close.

How long this continued
is hard to know.
Perhaps it is still happening.
Perhaps this is what I am feeling even now.
Do you see what you have done?
Do you think I will ever forget?

THE LOST ADULT

Here I sit, still chewing
the pith of my hoarded sufferings,
my remembered griefs,

now they are parts of my bones and cells,
they have integrated into my blood,
become my organs
of sight and feeling.
I would not give them up for any sum, these constant sweet
reminders
of my agony,
the shape and sinew of my soul:
Nothing feeds me like my pain.

THE SAINT

is mad for rapture.
She has learned
to endure
the passion of the god.
She yearns for epiphany,
to become nothing but ash.
She must be cautious, or she may die
like Danae, in a dream of gold,
or the Renaissance man who expired
from an "excess of joy":
I and My Beloved are one.

THE AWAKENED ONE LEAVES

Light passes to light,
all passion stilled.
Long ago I saw and surrendered, entered the beam
of the single eye.

I chose Nothingness
as my companion
and knew that loss,
like love, could not be held.
The only moment is that
pierced by the Other:
Now I go to become my own bride.

ON MY EIGHTIETH BIRTHDAY

I will, yes,
know everything,
seed to tree,
bole to blossoming,
what begins in joy
and ends in pain,
the moment lost in
time's hurricane,
the interlude engraved on the heart,
the one who was faithful,
the one who failed,
all of it
eaten like a dark blessing,
a sweet wafer soothing
the tongue.

ON YOUR SLENDER BODY

On your slender body
you wore what women wore then—
not silk, but jeans,
long white shirt,
hair parted behind.

You came in humming a song,
up to date, like you.
Your Indian eyes were brown,
distanced,
as if you were looking
at a secret,
something far away.

You were like a scent
hovering nearby,
perfuming the room,
saying,
Here I am. I've come.

We did nothing exceptional.
Sometimes we played bridge
with the others
in the living room,
or shared a meal
with them.

We seldom went places together.
Everything centered
on the one room, ours.
Something there
carried us
to yet another place.

I keep wondering
what happened to you,
where you went,
how many lovers you had
afterward.
Was it true,
as the newspaper said,
you had married?
It was hard to believe
and I wondered why.
Where are you now?
Do you still sing those throaty songs,
like love strokes in the dark?
I still have your picture.

This poem is inspired by another written in the nineteenth century by Wu Tsao, who has been called China's great lesbian poet. Her poem is one of longing for her beloved, an elegant courtesan. It begins "On your slender body/ Jade and coral girdle ornaments chime."

THE CELEBRITY LOVER

I knew from the
first
that you were only
temporary:
lover who climbs in
through the window
at midnight,
leaves before dawn.

You never made
any promises,
swore no vows.
In fact, you never even
touched me.

But I knew your
pattern.
How many you had
dazzled with your blazing talents,
wooed with precious gifts,
and then abandoned and
left behind
like yesterday's leftover fish.
The blazing star
who leaves a
score or more weeping
in his wake,

path strewn
with broken hearts.

So when you left
my heart was not
shattered.
I did not wail and pour ashes
on my head.
I did not grieve
in public,
didn't even tell
my best friend.

Still, sometimes
I miss you.
Wonder where you
went, what you are doing
now, your latest conquest.
If I will ever see you again.

(Note: the above poem is intended not only for those who have been
betrayed by their human loves, but also for those who have been "seduced,"
then abandoned by those they admired, such as teachers, mentors, gurus,
and such.)

IF YOUR HEART

If your heart has not been
burnt to cinders,
how can you know
the taste of the flame?

If you have not drowned
in the ocean of love,
how can you measure
the embrace of the abyss?

If you have not felt
God's kiss on your mouth,
how can you find
the death which is life?

IT IS TIME

I think it is time to remember
our wildness,
like the ancient women of Greece.
To take off our clothes
and run through the forest,
and let the trees brush
over our skin,
feel its rough scars,
its tender bruises,
and look the animals
in the eye,
naked to naked,
return growl for growl,
to claim the stars
as our own
as if we had made them
and placed them there
in their turning wheels,
and recite songs in trance
and find someone to love.

Now at last
I have become
Buddha.

That is to say,
When I bow
And close my eyes
Before his image,
I see myself sitting
As he does,
Lotus pose,
Eyes shut,
Hands arranged
In delicate mudra.

I move a bit,
Feel soft energies
stir within.

Soon it will be time
To turn
To doing—
Things to be emptied,
Things to be filled,
Walks outside
To greet the new fallen snow
Weighting the boughs
With their heavy love.

PART 5

From Unmasking the Rose

A RECORD OF A KUNDALINI INITIATION
2002

THE SUPPLICANTS

At the throne of God, the angels have no form at all,
but come as pure, raw energy. . .
—Sophy Burnham

There are many ways
of approaching the throne.

Some move solemnly,
majestically,
a procession of wise men
contemplating a final reality.

For others, it is a celebration
of the soul in love trance.
They are caught in a
fiery transformation,
a dancing beyond the reach
of silence or the Word.

Others quietly abase themselves,
moving forward slowly, intent,
imprinting the dust
again and again
with their bodies' thin shadows
as they go.

A GOLDEN HAZE OR HALO

I know you are there, waiting to find me,
to take me in your heavy jaws,
to gulp me like a morsel
or cough me up
like a briar.

For I am covered in thorns.
No, that's not so.
I am slicked over, oiled,
like something disguised
for a celebration.
I have made myself
an easy prey,
something to be quickly swallowed
and digested
or else
spat out in disgust.

You keep calling,
I keep looking the other way,
I beg my responsibilities,
my serious obligations.
You hear none of my
protestations,
they are irrelevant, weightless as air.

You sit back on your great haunches,

swish your tail,
make a warning growl in your throat.
I no longer remember how long
you have been there,
when you came.
Each time I scanned the landscape,
you are always what I saw.
Your mane floats like a golden haze or halo
around your unfathomable face.
Now you are pacing again.

PREPARING TO GREET THE GODDESS

Do not think of her
unless you are prepared
to be driven to your limits,
to rush forth from yourself
like a ritual bowl overflowing
with sacramental wine.

Do not summon her image
unless you are ready to be blinded,
to stand in the flash
of a center exploding,
yourself shattering into the landscape,
wavering bits of bark and water.

Do not speak her name
until you have said good-bye
to all your familiar trinkets—
your mirrors, your bracelets,
your childhood adorations.
From now on you are nothing,
a ghost sighing at the window,
a voice singing underwater.

MEETING WITH SILENCE

Why should I fall into you,
backwards spiral into nothingness, empty of words, images gone
as if dissolved in an acid bath?

You say, so that I may meet with Brahman,
face turned to facelessness,
confronting "bliss of the real,"
sans quality, without sound.

I say, for centuries I labored
to mass this body, shape this breast.
What flows through me a current
of my own devising,
even now the molecules ping their secrets,
blood-tones shimmering
their shameless joy.

WHO MOVE AMONG US

At midnight
in silence
we press
the dark oil
of our life's meaning
from a hundred nights of pain,
limitless days of dying.

What is joy
if not union
with the god
or else unbearable intensity of longing?
What is sorrow
but a glance imploring
that silent face?

Angels, I know you move
constantly among us
your stirring wings, your soft embrace—
we sense your nearness...
how can we withstand
such blood-driven tokens
of your insistent call?

RUINED BY YOUR BEAUTY

First, you cleansed me,
arriving as fire, as savage flood.

Next you tore me,
your panther tooth,
your lion claw,
limbs scattering like grass
in the garden of a great wind.

Then you made love to me,
night after night of unendurable
torment and passion.

Ruined by your beauty,
I have vanished,
fled into the nothingness
of who I am.

LISTENING TO MUSIC IN POSES

You have been tuned
for this moment
for a thousand years.
Each star at midnight,
each drop from the well
became who you are,
this vessel of anguished rapture:
flesh, muscle, bone.

Once there was a divine pulsation in heaven.
You and all that is
are its unfoldment,
summoning the world to being.

Listen.
Your blood knows how to be with
this dark intensity,
this opened vein of love,
like a flowing stillness before a storm,
a river moving quietly
through a hurricane.

It is beginning once more.

Imagine a Buddha
with light around
her head.
Her ear, the one
you are sleeping in.
Her breath,
the rhythm of your sleep,
your body her sounding board.

You are the one she has come for.
Now is your moment of honey and fire.

You sit in the midst
of your silence.
The world tide recedes,
taking even your name.
You cry out as the light
enters your heart.

LOVE TAKES US INTO ITS HOLY GROUND

Who was I, that such a thing
should happen
An ordinary woman,
living an unremarkable life
until a presence appeared
a being from some other
place or planet not found on any map,
reality without an image or a name.

Then you entered me and stayed,
a constant element like blood throbbing
through a vein
or light flowing
through all the secret chambers
of the heart
each cell and particle awakened
by your relentless call.

Now I am a no thing
a naked enterprise of love,
a relic on a ravaged field,
its essence swallowed by this clear light,
this transparent flaming joy.

RISHIS

What they knew
was that life
is not a pure exposition
of darkness, or light,
but a compendium,
a constantly shifting
blend,
as if from a master of chiaroscuro
who wanted to try all
the possible combinations
and angles,
gradations and permutations
of depiction
before declaring balance,
and then not stasis,
but the delicate harmony
of chaos, where everything streams
each shifting molecule,
each flowing strand of transitoriness
straining toward fulfillment
not through gaudy symmetry
but from the hidden skein
of a tangled, crafty design.

PART 6

New Poems

START WITH ROSES

Start with roses.
No matter if they have become
almost a cliché
available in
every garden.

Don't worry that every bride
and bridesmaid
that you have ever known
carried them up the aisle.

Don't fret that often divas receive
huge armfuls from the stage.

Sometimes whole gardens
are nothing but roses.
On certain occasions,
their petals are strewn
over the dead.

Roses have many meanings:
Christ in cathedral windows,
the final secret for those
who dabble
in occult realms.

For Dante, the rose was the emblem
of heaven itself.

Go there,
become a rose.

SIGNS IN THE SKY
(inspired by Lynn Ungar)

I am not one
for seeking signs
in the sky,
for skrying into plates
shimmering with water,
or discovering stones
on the path
with secret symbols,
directions to heavenly realms.

Yet when I go forth
and find these blinding
colors of fall—
indigo, vermillion, bronze—
entering my screen of seeing,
piercing me
with yearning always for more,
of knowing the world
around me, as something
I lack words to describe,
but can only say
(in a measured whispered tone),
Yes, yes,
this is what I meant,
what a perfect combination,
seer and seen united,
whatever it is
already come
down and entering where I am,
is this not a blessing?

BEFORE GALILEO

You think you are
the center of everything—
Those planets and galaxies
their dizzy spirals
and loops,
their constant circling around
endless space—
You imagine they are a light show
constructed for your benefit—
and you are at the very midpoint,
the way Earth itself was
before Galileo set us straight.

What indeed would you do
if this proved to be the case?
Would you tilt this way and that
to see if your universe went off center
with you?
Would you shrink into an atom
to see if your world would follow,
miniaturize itself?

Listen, there are a thousand billion
universes out there
and you are just a tiny speck
on one exceedingly small rounded sphere
hurling itself out into the immensity.

You suppose that your moods and
intuitions guide everything
around you,
that you are the creator
of endless voyagings and arrivals—
that you are the molecule
that defines all existence,
for the currents of the universe
flow constantly through you—
and they do,
they do,
and you are,
you are.

THE MOMENT WHICH CHANGES EVERYTHING

By now, we all know it
by heart,
that scientific tale of the
reputed cat in its theoretical box
which could be anything—
black or spotted,
here or there,
dead or alive—
until someone popped
off the lid and
peered inside,
and voila! there she was
a real cat
in all of her feline glory,
snowball or tiger,
prancing bronze or calico,
already purring for food.

Think about your life.
How, one day,
after so much continued repetition
of the weary familiar,
the unexpected happens,
something strange and startling,
which takes over and becomes
the leitmotif of your life,
the Dominant Theme,

all possibilities collapsed into a single
grain of expectation.
Everything thereafter
is colored by its hue.

This is called
the moment that changes everything.

WHAT WILL YOU DO

What will you do with the last good days?
— Lynn Ungar

Who was it that asked,
What if this present were the world's
last night?

Do you remember John Donne,
man of cloth and prayer?
Renegade clergy
who counseled us,
seek not for whom the bell
tolls, and then added the
disquieting answer?

At the bottom of the sea,
a hundred lost cities
lie buried in sand.
No one knows their purpose
or even their names.
Some men of learning
even doubt that they
existed.

Each morning we wake
and, like performers
on a tight rope,
take our long staves

and go forth.
To fall either way
is annihilation,
either into despair
or immeasurable joy.
Which will you choose,
now at the end of choosing,
now that the final choice is
standing before us,
wearing its mottled uniform,
its reminder of necessity,
love and fear together mixed?

ON THIS MUSIC

Why not give up
and become that which
it is?
Why not surrender totally,
flow into these vibrations,
swirl with these frequencies?
Angels can do it.

Where did these sounds come from?
Where did you?
Did someone discover the original
merger,
the source where we and it
(all of it, all of us)
were one,
one strong note,
one syllable, a single tone,
before we got parceled out,
separated into segments,
was this what is meant by
the fall?

WHO WENT UNHEARD

I think again and again
of those who went
so long unheard,
or even ignored.

Vivaldi and the children,
some hardly bigger
than their instruments.
Almost nobody really noticed.
No one really cared.
Yet they played on.

And dear Emily,
her letter to the world—
something kept her writing,
packets bound together in yarn,
poems in mittens
dropped for passing school children.

And of course Mozart,
his reward
the pauper's grave.
Who knows where he
entered earth?
All transmuted
to sound.

And even Bach,
out of favor at the end.

Blake and his angels,
Van Gogh in his madness,
Dante in exile...the list goes on.

One likes to believe
that in the other realm
these were at last fully heard,
vibrant voices circulating among
the angelic choirs,
choruses of Gloria
and string quartets
and the audience ravished—silent—
becoming only this.

SCARLET BERRIES

(Inspired by Rosemerry Wahtoma Trommer)

When I look at the scarlet berries,
necklace of beads adorning the leaves
of the branches above
and those fallen below,
let me not ponder their genus
or lineage,
their uses, or history.
Let me admire their glistening skin,
the way they turn to the sun at morning,
and hide their delicate faces in the night.

And when the moon comes forth
in the darkness
of the summer sky,
let me not worry about the true distance
between our world and it,
or how much it possibly weighs,
or when white-suited men will come once more
to plant their flags
above its surface.

When I follow the oak-lined trail
through the forest grove,
let me not pause to calculate
the square feet of lumber
their corpses might provide,

the "profits" their "owners"
might gain.

Nor carry a book to memorize
the names of all the many things
and creatures I meet on the way—
flowers golden and amethyst,
the small beings scurrying away,
the grasses singing in the undergrowth,
the birds soaring overhead,
heading somewhere.

The history of these mountains,
with their immeasurable tranquility.
The clouds dragging their white shawls
across the blue scrim of the sky.

Let me breathe the presence of each,
know it for another of who I am,
drink deeply of this stillness.

FOR MICHAEL BLACK, AGAIN

Now that he is gone,
I keep making him
into an angel

the gentleness.
the compassion.

How can someone
never speak ill
of another?
Or embrace without question
things the rest
of us merely wonder about?
(Are there really
angels waiting
in the wings,
ready to heal?)

What does it mean
to actually embody
"unconditional love"
no matter who or what
you may have done?

To respect each one
you meet, regardless
of circumstance?
I know he had his aggravations,
his tendency to go beyond the limits,

break the barriers,
voyage too far in the minds of many.

Did he really once live on Lemuria?
Was he in fact the reincarnation
of that famous ancient sage?

He couldn't even
keep a job,
always finding reasons to leave.

The original child.

And those incredible
puns—
outrageous by any standard.
And the ever growing
treasure horde of crystals
vibrating together like
one great bliss machine
and the voyages to other realms—
planets and stars
such as Sirius and Andromeda—
places we had barely heard of.

Always I see him
with this glow
surrounding his form,
even a suggestion of wings,
telling reminders
of who he was,
what he became.

OUR TIME

A man doesn't have time
to have time for everything.
—Yehudi Amachi

Frankly, I have given up
trying to comprehend it—
or measure it or define it
or capture it, even in
small moments.

Yes, there was only recently
the view from the height
of the snow-hung peaks
in the distance,
and for a small second
everyone fell silent
and we gazed in wonder without
trying to describe it
or discern whether or not it
had meaning.

They say that all time is
present in every moment—
that there is no past or present
or future,
that our own small awareness spreads
these out in order to grasp
the incomprehensible.

But nonetheless my mirror
tells a different story.
I know "my time" is finite,
that having come into this realm
at a specific moment
I will likewise depart when
"it is my time."

Something—events, transactions—
will occur when I am gone
and they will be meaningful
at the time.
Others will arrive
and find time
for their own inner destinies,
sadness and joy.

In the meantime,
I will manage,
find time to do what has to
be done,
leave the rest
for another time.

LALITA

I was never a priest
who stood in the temple
and repeated words
calling down God.

I was a little
girl child
who danced
in the dust
before my house.

One day Shiva
came,
took me in
his arms.

After that,
I did not care.
Household,
family
all drifted away.

All I wanted
was to dance
with what
had entered
my body.

They speak of me still.

ONLY IF SHIVA

Yes, there was a Moment
the sky flew open in a brilliant flash,
Shiva's eye opening,
and I was present,
the observer.
Torrents of thunderbolts
all the vajras of heaven
unlocking, nada brahma, the silent word,
but what do I know
I saw but what can I say about
such things.

If you are seeking
explanations and prescriptions,
then study lost ancient languages,
rummage primal texts.
You will find phrases you can intone,
gestures to repeat at sunrise and dusk
through years of yearning,
eons of striving to shatter time.

But only if Shiva nods you alive
will you enter the first moment
when the sky tears open
and Earth shudders,
creation exploding,
the beginning of the dance.

MAYBE SOMEWHERE

Maybe somewhere there is a monk
chanting
even though he lived
many years before
our time
began.

He is still there
saying his mantra,
Padmasambava listening,
sacred syllables
reverberating
his flesh.

Sound ascending,
nada brahma.
Hands turning,
Face of light.

THE BUDDHA WITHIN

The Buddha who is you
is kissing you inside.
The Buddha who is you
is filling your body with light.

Open always to the light.
Let your body,
each filament and cell,
shine with the Luminous One,
the immaculate being
who is who you are.

TIBETAN, RESONANT

At first it was a great organ,
resounding all the notes
of my body, making a bright song
of my flesh and inner realms.

Then it became a bell,
Tibetan, resonant,
awakening me everywhere,
sounding God in my body.

Now it is more like light
playing over a surface
of water,
the sun glinting over
reflections of itself,
mountains snow clad
and brilliant,
shining white
within the lake's dark waters.

HOW IT IS

Don't tell me that when the angels
listen to Bach (*say his Concerto for Clavier
Violin, and Viola*) –they don't dance around
in heavenly spirals,
become their ultimate selves,
Or when Brahms' *German Requiem* begins to play,
that they don't move in procession
around the throne,
ranks and files
in proper order.

How else account for that sweet honey
that flows down to us
when the music
begins to play?

How explain
what it is
that then enters
and claims us?

For a moment
We, too, float above
as if we were
angels alongside
the others.
For a brief time
we are more.

ONE OF THE WAYS

It is one of the many ways to enter fire.
— Mary Oliver

And, yes, we enter,
either by our own volition
or the command of the gods.

And then we flare,
a small frenzy of color,
until we are finished—
a glowing silhouette,
ready for what awaits—

the sunlit music of the world
with its insistent curves
and turnings,
or else
a withdrawal,
the all-consuming silence
that comes only
to those
who have known
the flames.

FLOODING AND BLIND
(Dedicated to all who have had sudden, unexpected spiritual awakening)

The problem is that
before,
we did not pretend to
know anything,
just cautious groping in
the dark,
occasional glimpses
of a dimming light,
music distantly heard.

Then, after it happened,
we did know,
not with words
but with feeling,
bliss flooding and blind,
carrying us where
there was no real evidence
that could be proved,
only the mute testimony
of the blood.

WHO SHE IS

I would not say
that She was Kali.
I would not say
that She was not Kali.

I would not say
that She was Tara.
I would not say
that She
was not Tara.

I would not say
that She was the
Mother of All That Is.
I would not say
that She
was not the Mother
of All That Is.

I would say only,
"She is the one
who comes."

Sometimes She
is male,
sometimes She
is female.

Sometimes She
is both
or neither.

I know Her only
by Her presence.

Her presence is
called My Beloved,
and when She arrives,
She becomes
who I am.

Now that you have
destroyed me,
oh, my Beloved,
what am I to do with
my life?

I try to listen
to the sayings
of the savants and
wise men,
but everything seems
like something
I know already,
and don't need to be
told again.

I try to follow the practices
in the books,
but these are dull,
heavy like bread that never rose—
they don't take me
anywhere, leave me
stranded between
ennui and despair.

The Shakti, the love thrilling
the veins,

Where is it? I ask,
and turn the page.

Only when I am with you,
my Dear One,
only when we are alone,
silence knitting us
together as one being,
only then am I
complete.

WHEN SHE CAME

When She came
I did not know
what was going to happen.

That I would have to give up
everything
and become a pauper at the gate.

Now I have no name,
no identity,
no function in this world
other than to be with Her.

She, too, arrived
without name
or form.

Now we are twins,
always together,
honey dissolved in wine.

FOR SO VERY LONG

For so very long
I told no one
about our secret love making,
a hidden honeymoon.

Then one day
I sang my song
and sent it
into the world.

Now the echoes return to me
from many directions,
the melody translated
again and again.

ROUGH BARK

Yes, I know,
I have been blessed
with delight beyond measure,
light playing
over lips and eyes,
surging through the veins,
no known triggers,
not repetition of
sound
nor postures
nor solicitation
of celestial visions.

Yet there are times
when I long
for that which is more palpable:
the feel of rough bark
against my palm,
drift of clouds through
the purple of twilight,
red hibiscus blooming
in a private garden.

Some say this is a preview
of what lies beyond,
that we will all taste it
in that other realm.

They call it
bodiless love.

THESE WORDS

What are these words
woven into
the tapestry of my
body?

What shall I do
now that I am become
a piece torn from
an unknown script?

What music plays
through the instrument
that is who I am?

How is it that I am become
a song
whispered into God's ear?

FOOL'S GOLD

Who am I that I must always be pretending,
Never showing all of
who I am?

If you are not ready,
do not seek to know this
treasure.

You will only discover
fool's gold
and proclaim,
"This secret revelation
is in fact a fraud!
Don't believe a word
of what they say."

THE WINEMAKERS

The winemakers claim that only they
know how to brew,
that age itself
is the key
to the celestial drink.
But some of us
could not wait—
we got dead drunk
on the first sip.

AFTER THAT

After that
everything
changes.

As if you
walked into
a familiar room,
chairs, mirrors
all in place
yet something is different—
colors deepened to
a more lustrous hue,
the light moving
in unexpected patterns,
waves dissolving,
even the music
that you know so well
playing in a new key.

YOUR BODY

Your body, Her body,
they are one.

Your lips,
Her lips,
are the same.

When you breathe in,
Her breath of roses
comes into your lungs.
When you breathe out,
Her scent
fills the room.

Even when you look
in the glass,
it is Her face you see.

THE OFFERING

I have placed my heart
on this altar,
and now the animals come
one by one—
the lion,
the leopard,
even the hyena—
each taking their share.

They have arrived
to consume,
devour,
deliver me where
their own most
secret meaning abides:
cells and blood,
hide and bone.

Listen and you can
hear my voice calling
in their roar.
How I float
from sinew to
sinew.
How I drift
among the
hidden currents

of their veins.

At times I wonder,
Who have I become?
How much rapture can I bear?

IS IT THE NIGHT OF BECOMING?
*(Modeled after a poem by Bibi Hayati,
early 19th century female Sufi poet)*

Is it the night of becoming,
or only the touch of your hand
across my face?

In the manuscript of awakening,
is it the key words
or only the shadow
of your pen?

Is it the roses
blooming
in the secret garden
or only the pines
rising before you?

Is it the perfume
of the forest
or the scent of
the breeze that carries you?

Is it the mountain lightening,
whitening the landscape
or the brilliant rays
of your eyes?

My longing and sighing
or the steady beat of your heart?

Is it the wine of
a ritual celebration
or the intoxication
of your presence?
Is it your all-seeing vision
or the magic you weave
when you come?

Is this a hallowed sanctuary
or a place of ignorant passion?
Is it the moment of union
or only a mistaken dream?

Always I seek
to be close to you,
longing to see
your hidden face.

ZEN POEM

Long journey.
No guide.
Many deserts and mountains,
peaks and valleys.
Finally arrived home.
Almost knew where I was.

AFTER KABIR

I am not here,
I am not there.

I am bird flying toward the sun
and fish swimming in the depths.

I do not walk on two legs,
nor gallop on four.

I am the circle
and its hidden center.

I am the pleasure
and also the pain.

I am God peering down
on Earth
and the petitioner searching the sky
for the One.

I am the poet writing
and also the poem.

I am the book
and the reader turning its pages.

I am the tongue

and the words it speaks.

I am the god of stillness
and the goddess moving within.
I am myself
and the you I met in the street last night.
I have no name
and am the sound that is uttered
by the saint.

I do not live here
and am never home at my address.

I am the lost soul
and the awakened worshipper.

KRISHNA TO ARJUNA

Those who desire me
follow in my footsteps
even as these disappear
into the snow.

Those who give me
their love
will be cherished,
as a rare fruit
is sweet
in the mouth.

Those who know me
will be silent
even in the midst
of wisdom sayers
who have little to say.

LISTENING

Yes, what I want is God talk,
words whispered into my ear,
streaming over me
like rose petals
falling from the clouds.

Syllables soothing me,
telling me
that indeed it is there,
whole and holy,
the thing we reach for,
the prize we want
and will have,
no matter what.

ORPHEUS

The way the music bathes you.

The way it seizes you
and does not let go.

How enraptured we become.

How we do not remember the
other time, when there were two of us,
and not just one,
a single fused reality

Do not talk to me
of something you call
"non-dual."

Let your words cease
and listen in silence,

and know union.

THE SKEPTICS

We were the skeptics,
the ones who knew
that nothing exists
beyond our knowing,
our certitude that what we saw
was what there was,
no need to go
beyond the edges
of our thought,
our need to be right.

Then one day
we were struck down
by Presence arriving
in a whirling cloud
of light,
a wind tearing
our clothes away,
our skin was now suffused with gold,
and we no longer remembered
what it was we knew.

DANCING GODS
(for Andrew)

Never trust a god who doesn't dance.
— Alain Danilou

Who are the dancing gods?

What is the name of those
who come to us and enter us
and make us splendid?

How is it
that they come so far
to be so close?

How is it that they
wish to claim us
and we wish to be
claimed,
ourselves
an altar of love?

When will they carry us
to the dancing ground
of the many nameless ones,
the great ones who ever
sing and dance together?

PRAYER ON A DAY OF BLISS

May the Energies of the Universe
flow through me.

May the sweetness of the gods
touch my lips.

May the strength of the guardians
come into my veins.

May I dwell in purity and love,
always.

May I offer all I have
to that which lives
inside and outside
of who I am.

I BECAME THE FISH

One raindrop fell
on my tongue
and I became the fish
who drowned in
the ocean
of light.

A rose opened.
I fell
into its core
and transformed into
the seed of all life.

The sun's rays
scorched
the desert sand
and burnt away all signs of awareness.
I bloomed silently below
and became the molecule
of the world
of living things
that exist
even amidst the dunes
and cinders.

STAGES

This is the final thing.
Power and faith, power and blood.
—Linda Gregg

Power and blood,
distilled in faith.
All of us came
down here in desire,
wanting.
The yielding nipple,
its fruity
offering.
The love spasm,
shuddering through
like a divine fury
striking.
Always we gave and received,
received and gave,
until we were weary of Things,
worn out with doing.
Interminable waiting,
endless despair.
Stricken searching in the dark.
Sudden illumination igniting
all the tapers
of the soul.
Veins and sinews lit
with incandescent joy.

HOW IT WILL BE

"When naked to naked goes..."
— Yeats

All translated
to music and light,
Final frequencies
And a drift of awareness.

Familiar,
like the taste of some fruit
you ate for breakfast
each morning,
the voice of an old friend,
someone you loved
singing as
she entered

But always approaching,
never fully arriving,
this music piercing
to the root,
light invading the nerves,
the skeleton
to the edge of feeling
rapture, rapture,
however it came
now the Beloved naked at last
pure, ultimate

HER DARK FACE

You want to know about the goddess?
She will come into your life, stealthily,
or else like an explosion of flame
from a great forest fire.

You will be torn to bits,
to pieces of love,
of imagining,
of grasping
and moaning.

She will rend you
piece by piece,
until you cry out with rapture,
until you cry for mercy
of forgiveness,
satiety of
joy.

You will dance with her
night after night,
never knowing
who she is,
who you are,
where you came from,
where you are going.

Always, her dark face
before you.

SHE

When I live in that woman,
she lives in me.

When I drink wine with that woman,
her lips touch the glass
I drink from.

When I come home at evening,
she is the one who waits for me.

Even now,
she is brushing her hair
in front of the glass,
laying out her nightclothes,
beckons me to bed.

JOURNEYS
(for the Beloved Within)

Some went to
India and Egypt
to seek the wonder.

They met the Sages,
entered the pyramids,
searching for the hidden treasure.

Not one to travel,
I did not explore
the sacred centers.

I stayed home and
felt the bliss.

You and I,
my darling—
we made love
together
for so many days,
endless nights.

Our journey ended
in each other.

APPENDIX

The following piece by Andrew Harvey was originally included as the introduction for the first edition of Marrow of Flame. It is reprinted here with his permission in order to provide a context for the poems in this volume.

Introduction for Marrow of Flame, First Edition

Andrew Harvey

Some years ago now I gave classes on Rumi at the California Institute of Integral Studies. After one of them, during my office hours, a gentle and shy woman with short cropped gray hair in her early sixties came in to talk to me. Before she even began to speak, I was startled by the kind clarity of her presence, the unmistakable aura of canny and tried goodness that clothed her. We spoke of many things that afternoon—about Rumi and his extraordinary relationship with Shams, about the nature of mystical ecstasy, about the kind of rigor and capacity for ordeal demanded by the authentic path of transformation; it became clear to me very quickly that I had a great deal to learn from the woman sitting before me, and that she spoke not from curiosity, or even literary or spiritual passion, but from the most profound, intricate and seasoned inner experience. What struck me most that afternoon about Dorothy Walters was her humility; unlike many of my Californian students and friends, she did not claim enlightenment or flaunt her "mystical" insights. Part of her, I felt, was always kneeling in silence before the vastness of the mystery that had clearly claimed her for its own: she spoke of the Divine haltingly, and with a refined and poignant tenderness, like a lover of her Beloved. And she had a wild Irish laugh, too, which reassured me.

In the years since, we have become the greatest and deepest of friends and I have come to think of Dorothy as a spiritual mother and as one of the few true mystics I have met in my life. Her beauty of soul has illumined my life; her courage has inspired me always to travel deeper into my own vision; I have been able to speak to her, as a fellow seeker and lover of God, with complete candor about the demands of the Path. When I left Meera in circumstances that caused great scandal and controversy, Dorothy wrote me a letter which I shall always cherish and re-read often in which she begged me to "remain true to myself whatever happens and never to give in to any of the terrible pressures my actions and insights will inevitably arouse." It was the perfect advice, perfectly expressed, at exactly the right time; this kind of precision characterizes Dorothy's spirit. The only other being who in my experience combined such deep kindness with such wisdom was Iris Murdoch; one of the great sadnesses of my life is that Iris died before they could meet. When I think of them together I think of the commentary the I Ching gives on the sixth line of the hexagram Ting, The Cauldron. "The Ting has rings of jade." "Jade is notable for its combination of hardness with soft luster...here the counsel is described in relation to the sage who imparts it. In imparting it, he will be mild and pure, like precious jade."

It was only after the first two years of our friendship that Dorothy began, diffidently and self-deprecatingly, to show me the poems she was writing. I was immediately struck by them; they were exquisitely made, subtle, passionate and profound, unlike anything else I knew that was being written in our time. Whenever we met, Dorothy would bring some fresh works to our meeting. Slowly, as we read them together and discussed them, Dorothy came to reveal more to me of her remarkable inner journey; a journey that has led her through much ordeal and heartbreak and loneliness from a cramped and sometimes difficult childhood, through a long, testing stint as a teacher of literature and women's studies in a Midwestern university, to the festive and fertile spiritual and personal life she enjoys now in her very active "retirement" in San Francisco, surrounded by books and music and friends.

Three years ago I summoned up my courage and asked Dorothy to write to me and describe her mystical voyage in her own words. This is part of what she wrote:

> For most of my life, I have sought ways to be in touch with what is sometimes called the Mystery—the truth that underlies the appearance of the many things, the reality that provides the hidden basis for the manifest world of the senses. In childhood I experienced this connection on a deep intuitive level in the world of nature. I lived close to open fields and gentle rolling woodlands. Each excursion into these precincts was, for me, an entry into terrestrial paradise.

In her letter, Dorothy goes on to describe how, in her adolescence, she went through what she calls her "first" spiritual conversion.

> In adolescence, I discovered Emerson and Thoreau as

well as Plato's myth of the cave. These spoke to me on a profound level, and, under the guidance of a highly spiritual teacher of transcendental literature, I underwent a classic Christian conversion. I felt a renewal akin to rebirth and saw the world with cleansed eyes. Love, grace and beauty suffused all which lay about, including the most common objects—pebble, leaf and stone. The universe revealed itself as a reflection of divine intelligence, and all things conspired for ultimate good.

This early conversion experience dimmed, however, during Dorothy's graduate school years—the first of many spiritual "deaths" that she has weathered.

From 1953 to 1960 I was a student of English and American literature at a Midwestern university, at a time when women were not encouraged to pursue advanced degrees. Like most of my colleagues I embraced a more "intellectual" approach, adopting an elitist skepticism which challenged whatever was not subject to rational inquiry and investigation.

This "skeptical intellectual" approach began to crumble during the 60's and 70's when Dorothy became established as a university professor in English and women's studies. As she wrote to me:

"In the 60s and 70s, I began to read widely in psycho-spiritual literature, some of which was just emerging: Carlos Castaneda and Carl Jung, Joseph Campbell, Mircea Eliade... and especially the poetry and occult writings of W.B. Yeats. I delved into the workings of the Golden Dawn and read and re-read Evelyn Underhill's classic writings on mysticism. This background helped to awaken in me a sense of psychic reality beyond the bounds of ordinary consciousness and in my forties I underwent a fairly explosive psychic opening.

This "fairly explosive psychic opening" led Dorothy to experience telepathic communication, the reality of auras and inner lights and visions, and included "contact with a specific spiritual guide." She studied tarot, astrology and Kabbalah, and engaged in Ouija work and quasi-automatic writing. The poetry she had always written casually now became focused on the inner journey, "drawing inspiration from the archetypal images of both the goddess and the hero."

Her esoteric investigations disturbed her however:

> I ceased to explore them further after one particularly unsettling experience. (Who were these forces really? Where had they come from? Was there any truth to their pronouncements, any purpose to these manifestations?) For the next seven years I shunned occult realms and wrote primarily on academic themes.

This "shunning of occult realms" for seven years did not however "shut down" Dorothy's inner journey; in fact, it seems to have been the mysterious prerequisite for the experience which she acknowledges as having been the determining illumination of her life. This is how she describes in her letter what happened to her:

> In 1981 I experienced an inner emotional crisis which culminated in an abrupt, profound and totally transfiguring Kundalini awakening. One Sunday morning, in late May, I was reading in my living room in the Midwestern university city where I taught; the sun was streaming in through my high clerestory windows, the elm-lined street was quiet. I was now fifty-three years old, and facing the imminent breakup of a long term relationship. To me the prospect was devastating, more than I could bear to contemplate. Once again I had failed to achieve a permanent relationship. Once more I was undergoing a kind of spiritual death...
> The book I was reading that day mentioned Kundalini but did not describe it in detail. It spoke of the ancient yogis who could raise the "serpent power" from the base of the spine to the head. On impulse, I decided to see if I could lift my own energies this way. I meditated on an image of the god and goddess in union (from an illustration in the text) and focused on my breathing. Almost instantaneously I felt a great surge of ecstatic energy in the lower chakras and then, within seconds, this intense force rushed upward and into my head. My very crown seemed to open in rapture, and, for many minutes, I felt the energies of the unseen immensity flow in, as if petal after radiant petal were

unfolding in my crown. As long as I did not think about what was happening, the experience continued, but each time self-awareness intruded, the process was interrupted.

In that moment of grace, I realized that the notion of personal identity was an ongoing illusion, a myth the small being recites to itself in its state of lostness and isolation. I knew that we were each one but atoms within the larger frame, the boundless real...I did not return immediately to ordinary consciousness. I remained in a state of exalted awareness and rapture for months thereafter. I seemed to undergo a prolonged initiation directed by unseen inner guides...I saw the light around my body and heard my new name.

Everything was now lit by an inner beauty surpassing everything I had experienced before. Every face was my own, every leaf or bloom an aspect of my being. I felt that I had, at last, fused all levels; I knew, finally and incontrovertibly, that spirit and flesh are one, matter and the transcendent but differing faces of a single essence.

In the almost twenty some years since her Awakening, Dorothy has undergone a great deal of battering physical and mental stress; as all those who have experienced an overwhelming arousal of the Kundalini know, it can take decades of humble, often baffling inner work for its initiations to begin to be integrated in body and spirit. Perhaps the greatest difficulty Dorothy experienced, especially at the beginning, was her isolation; her "Awakening" occurred when she was teaching in Wichita, Kansas, a place not noted for its proliferation of free-thinking mystics.

Joining any kind of sect or putting herself under the guidance of a guru was foreign to Dorothy's temperament; From very early on, Dorothy told me once, I knew that I would have to travel alone. A part of me rejoiced; another part of me almost fainted away with terror.

Despite all difficulties and obstacles, however, through all the minor and major ordeals of the transformation she has submitted herself to, Dorothy has kept doggedly faithful to the supreme lessons her Awakening taught her. Now in her early seventies, she has, I believe, achieved a rare and high fusion of her feminine and masculine energies, of wisdom and compassion, gravity and delight, inner prayer and outer service. She is coming into what Rumi so beautifully calls "the Sea of Peace in which all ships find safety at long last." To be in her presence is to be in the presence of someone who has been through a long, sometimes terrible, hidden war and who has won through to an authentic, sober but electric radiance and the grace of God. The young girl finding the terrestrial paradise in the fields around her home has become the older woman increasingly at one with the Divine in all her movements, subtle actions, and tender humor.

I have explored Dorothy's wonderful journey here at some length because it everywhere illuminates Marrow of Flame. This unique book of poems is the record of the discoveries, visions, ordeals, and integrations of her long journey to Wholeness. Its mysterious authority springs directly from the intricate and lived depth, range, and passion of Dorothy's inner experience. The "voice " of Marrow of Flame—at once quiet and inexorable, gentle and wild, "feminine" in its intimacy and "masculine" in its power and sometimes brilliant certainty—is the voice of Dorothy herself, of Dorothy's transforming self; it is the voice of a person turning to gold through the long alchemy of Divine Love. The poems of Marrow of Flame are recognizably that of a modern woman and seeker; there is nothing archaic about their diction or presentation or sphere of reference; yet they are also timeless and often "sing" with the unnerving directness of the ancient mystical poets, such as Mechthild of Magdeburg, or Mirabai, or Ramprasad. What Dorothy has accomplished in this subtle and ravishing masterpiece is something that many modern poets have been struggling for but without success—a book of poems that work both as canny literary artifact and mystical utterance and inspiration. The years will reveal what a prophetic achievement this is.

There are three things I am especially grateful for in these poems. The first is their unfailing craft, the reward of decades of study of English and other literatures, and humble daily practice in different forms and genres. No one achieves so transparent and so sharply and exactly cadenced a living "voice" without immense work and literary acumen. Dorothy's command of all the "tricks" of the poet's trade—from buried half-rhymes to gorgeous and dazzling natural imagery to long, looping and overlapping melismas of syntax—is all the more impressive for being so "hidden;" at no point does "manner" ever overpower "substance." All her artifice as a "maker" is at the service of the higher and more important truths she knows and is trying to honor. She is far too enamored of the initiations of silence to over-privilege the games of language; yet the words of her finest poems shine with this silence, as the moon does, reflecting a secret sun.

The second aspect of Marrow of Flame that I am profoundly moved by and grateful for is what I can only call its "spiritual honesty." In a time of grotesque and vulgar mystic "hype" and inflation, the sometimes hesitant, exploratory clarity of the voice of these poems comes as the most vivid refreshment. Rumi used to say that you can tell an authentic mystic by the "sear-marks of the Flame of Love on their faces and hearts." Such "sear marks" are everywhere evident in Marrow of Flame. Dorothy has fought and suffered greatly, as most true mystics do, for her illumination, and can communicate to us—without frightening us—just how much the Quest costs and what resources of courage, self-knowledge, and abandon you have to summon from deep within yourself to be able to continue it. Repeated readings of Marrow of Flame will reveal to any sensitive reader what it represents: a massively experienced and accurate spiritual "autobiography," the record, shameless but unhysterical, of an extreme love affair with the Divine.

Unlike many modern so-called "mystics," Dorothy does not claim anything like total enlightenment, or parade her ecstasies as guaranteeing her any special election. She knows far too much not to know that the authentic journey is into a deeper and deeper humility, a greater and greater awe at the Divine, and has and can have no final "end" in this or any of the other worlds or dimensions. As Dorothy said to me once, "I have discovered that we are always traveling onward. The higher and further we travel, the lighter we become." These poems in Marrow of Flame have the transparent "lightness" of the "high" traveler; they wear their wisdom with the casualness of consummate tact.

The third power of these poems that I want to celebrate is their "initiatory intensity." They themselves are the crafted births of a prolonged and continual initiation into divine reality; their candor is the candor of the emerging Divine Self speaking of its discoveries directly. They not only incessantly invoke the Divine Light in all of its modes and operations but are saturated with its energy. Anyone who reads these poems with an open soul will find themselves being led, as if by the hand, into the depths of their own most profound visions, insights, dreams and revelations and will receive, almost without being conscious of it, the most vivid kind of inner encouragement.

As Dorothy writes in "Order of Melchizedek:"

Know who you are.

Do not debase the name.

Carry it in your heart,

a root flame of love.

Walk through the world in silence.

The moment will come.

This "initiatory intensity" of Marrow of Flame is all the more powerful, I believe, because it streams from the work of someone who does not in any way seek the status of a "master" or "great mystic." Dorothy's deepest wisdom--and the deepest wisdom of her poems--is that of an irradiated "ordinariness." She knows--and her poems show that she knows--that the greatest of all human achievements is to become one's own complete integrated divine human self in the core of ordinary life where, as she writes in "Still Life:"

Each movement,

each quiet gesture,

awakens

a rosary in the blood.

This knowledge of the inherent sacredness of "ordinary" reality pervades Marrow of Flame and grounds its ecstasies and wilder revelations. We trust Dorothy as a guide to the life of the spirit because she invites us at once to open up to the subtlest suggestions of the soul and to integrate them with our lives and duties. As she writes in her exquisite quatrain "Waiting:"

The jeweled cloud sways overhead

waiting.

Meanwhile, our cells are turning to air,

finer and finer arrangements of light.

For many years I thought I would be among only a handful of people who knew who Dorothy "is" and who can derive strength and joy from her. Now in Marrow of Flame she will make many new invisible soul-friends, and her profound illumination will go on living, long after she or I are dead, in the deathless Light that all souls live in and somewhere know as their origin.

AUTHOR'S NOTE

Dorothy Walters, Ph.D, spent most of her early professional life as a professor of English literature in various Midwestern universities. She helped to found one of the first women's studies programs in this country and served as the director of this program for many years. After an extended residence in San Francisco, she now lives and writes in Colorado, where she has a close relationship with the mountains as well as various streams and canyons.

She underwent major Kundalini awakening in 1981 (a phenomenon totally unfamiliar to her as well as to most of her contemporaries at the time); since then she has devoted her life to researching and writing about this subject and to witnessing the unfolding of this process within herself as well as assisting others on a similar path through writing and other means. As someone who made her extensive journey without the direction of any external leader or guru, church, or established order, she is a strong believer in the "guru within," the inner guide rather than the external authority figure or institution. The poems in this volume grow directly from that ongoing experience.

She feels that universal Kundalini awakening is the means for planetary and personal evolution of consciousness, and that evidence of planetary initiation is becoming more and more prevalent. Her poetry gives expression to the intense experiences of both the ecstasy and pain that Kundalini may bring as we undergo this inner transformation.

Her Kundalini awakening and subsequent process of unfolding are described in "Unmasking the Rose, A Record of a Kundalini Initiation." Her article on "Kundalini and the Mystic Path" is included in "Kundalini Rising," an anthology from Sounds True Publications. Her poems, which have been included in many anthologies and journals, have been set to music and sung at the Royal Opera House (seminar rooms) in London as well as Harvard University, Boulder's Resonance Chorus, and various choirs, used as texts for sermons and read aloud in churches, included in doctoral theses, been frequently quoted, and have given inspiration to many. Recently, a pilgrim to Petra read one of her poems aloud while there. Her newest book is a collection of poems called "The Kundalini Poems." These verses give expression to the experience of awakening into Kundalini, as it unites us with the Beloved Within.

Now in her 92nd year, she often gives counsel and referral free of charge to those undergoing spontaneous Kundalini Awakening and/or spiritual transformation.

A comprehensive online portal of her work is included as part of The Mystery School for a New Paradigm website and can be found by visiting www.DorothyWalters.com. There you will find recent YouTube videos featuring Dorothy and Andrew Harvey reading from her books Some Kiss We Want and The Kundalini Poems as well as his book Turn Me to Gold. Other videos focus on Dorothy's spiritual life and explorations of Kundalini Awakening. You will also find a link to her popular blog Kundalini Splendor.

Dorothy Walters is active on facebook and can be contacted directly at dorothywalters72@gmail.com.

SOME KISS WE WANT

(second edition)

.

www.ingramcontent.com/pod-product-compliance
Lightning Source LLC
Chambersburg PA
CBHW021500090426
42739CB00007B/402